Celtic
Christianity

Celtic Christianity

A Sacred Tradition, a Vision of Hope

TIMOTHY J. JOYCE, OSB

ORBIS BOOKS

Maryknoll, New York 10545

Second Printing, April 1998

The author wishes to acknowledge the gracious permission given by the following publishers to reprint copyrighted material:

T. & T. Clark Ltd., Publishers, for passages from Noel Dermot O'Donoghue and M. Forthomme Nicholson in *An Introduction to Celtic Christianity*, ed. James P. Mackey; Columba Press, Dublin, for use of Peter O'Dwyer's *Towards a History of Irish Spirituality*; the Continuum Publishing Company for prayers from *Celtic Christian Spirituality: An Anthology of Medieval and Modern Sources* © 1995 by Oliver Davies and Fiona Bowie; the Crossroad Publishing Company for excerpts from Thomas Day's *Why Catholics Can't Sing*; Four Courts Press, Dublin, and the University of Notre Dame Press for quotations from Liam De Paor, *Saint Patrick's World: The Christian Culture of Ireland's Apostolic Age*; Lindisfarne Books, Hudson, New York, for selections from Alexander Carmichael, *Carmina Gadelica: Hymns and Incantations*; Thames and Hudson, London, for quotations from Maire and Liam De Paor, *Early Christian Ireland* © 1958; Veritas Publications, Dublin, for quotations from *Irish Catholics: Tradition and Transition* © 1980 by John J. O'Riordain; and Weidenfeld and Nicolson, Ltd., London, for passages from Jacqueline O'Brien and Peter Harbison, *Ancient Ireland: From Prehistory to the Middle Ages*; Aureus Publishing, Cardiff, Wales, for verses from the oratorio, *Dewi Sant*; Constable Publishers, London, for quotation from Peter Berresford Ellis, *Celtic Inheritance*; Element Books Ltd, Dorset, England, for quotation from Anthony Duncan, *The Elements of Celtic Christianity*.

Library of Congress Cataloging-in-Publication Data

Joyce, Timothy J.
    Celtic Christianity : a sacred tradition, a vision of hope /
Timothy J. Joyce.
        p.   cm.
    Includes bibliographical references and index.
    ISBN 1-57075-176-5 (alk. paper)
    1. Celts – Religion. 2. Christianity and other religions – Celtic.
3. Ireland – Religion. 4. Celts. 5. Spirituality – Celtic Church.
    I. Title.
BL900.J68 1998
270'.089'916–dc21   97-44935
                                                              CIP

Contents

Preface

SINCE BEGINNING THIS WORK on Celtic Christianity I have been aware of the many books appearing on themes of Celtic culture, history, art, religion, and various related topics. While finding much that is delightful and instructive, I have nevertheless pursued my own particular interest and my desire to share what I have uncovered. It is my real hope that I can share the importance and significance of all this to me.

My own study of Celtic spirituality reflects a personal threefold perspective. I write as an Irish-American, as a Roman Catholic, and as a Benedictine monk. While the vast majority of what has been written on the subject has come from European centers, I write as an Irish-American. I was born and raised in New York City in a German-Irish neighborhood. My father was born in Brooklyn of Irish émigrés, both of whom died before I was born. My mother also came from Brooklyn, from a background of German-speaking Slovenian emigrants. Neither my father nor my mother spoke much of their own parents' background and they did not seem to know much about their European roots. They were typical first-generation Americans whose parents had been left behind and who tended to forget whence they had come. I never paid a great deal of attention to their ethnic backgrounds either. I thought of myself as an American. When told that I had the map of Ireland on my face, I would look in the mirror with some confusion and bewilderment. I guess there must also have been some fascination, however, as I can recall once marching in the Saint Patrick's Day Parade in New York. I also took Patrick as a patron saint for my Confirmation. My father died when I was twenty-six, and I, regretfully now, had never taken the opportunity to delve into his memories of his parents and their Irish background.

My early indifference disappeared when I had an awakening of awareness and interest in my Irish background. This occurred in

1978 when the Museum of Fine Arts in Boston hosted a special exhibition entitled "Treasures of Early Irish Art — 1500 B.C. to 1500 A.D." There I saw, exhibited in a historically organized display, an extraordinary collection of early Irish history. I gazed upon gold torques (collars) and jewelry, bronze cauldrons, ornate animal sculptures, crucifixion plaques, the "Tara Brooch," the Ardagh chalice, Saint Patrick's bell, bookshrines, the cross of Cong, the Stowe Missal, and the magnificent Book of Kells. My reaction was deep and immediate. Tears came to my eyes as I wondered what happened to this marvelous civilization and why I had not known anything about it. Why had "Irish culture" been for me a mush of cuteness, green beer, leprechauns, and maudlin tales about the "auld sod"? Something stirred within me, connecting me to a reality I had not previously recognized.

For twenty years now I have been pursuing this connection. I have sought to understand and appreciate what this ancient Irish civilization was all about. In this search I have uncovered deep layers of a wider "Celtic" culture and a Celtic church that was something far different than what my own church experience had taught me. Since then I have read numerous books and articles, attended conferences and lectures, listened to music, and shared with others who have the same interest. I have been to Ireland eight times and to Scotland once for the purpose of experiencing some of this heritage from within the midst of a living people.

Then, a few years ago, I gathered some of my insights together and started presenting workshops on "Celtic spirituality." These have taken on a life of their own as participants have responded with great fervor. Each one has taught me more and influenced the next presentation. By the touch of a provident God, the first workshop was attended by Mairead Loughnane Doherty, a Celtic harpist born in County Tipperary, Ireland. I asked Mairead to join me in presenting further workshops. She has added a great deal to these workshops and we have also developed a retreat on Celtic themes. Much of what I share in these pages has come from these Celtic weekend programs. Mairead reviewed the first draft of this book and made some helpful suggestions. In particular I thank her for the insights on the modern Irish woman, which she shares in our workshops and upon which I have based my portrait in chapter 6.

My second perspective comes from my being a Roman Catholic and an ordained priest. (My older brother, Tom, was a New York policeman, giving us the typical Irish-American "cop-and-priest" family profile.) The Second Vatican Council caused another awakening in my life, one of a religious and spiritual nature. It offered new life, new insights into being church and priest. I do not think we have yet begun to assimilate the vision of this great council. Looking at the experience of the Celtic church excites me, giving me an image of what the new church that God is moving us into could be. It also gives me a hint of what a more contemporary spirituality might look like. What I am sure of is that the forms of church and spirituality that were good for an immigrant church of the nineteenth century do not suffice for today. The council turned our eyes outward to a world we had feared and asked us to dialogue with it, without being swallowed up by it. The old, defensive, often negative ways do not bear fruit. But I can look further back in history and come to understand a tradition that is, indeed, old, but unbelievably new as well. While much that has been written about this tradition so far has come from non-Catholic, mainly Anglican, sources, I bring a Catholic perspective to it in these pages.

Finally I am a Benedictine monk. My monastic tradition is an ancient one, like the Celtic tradition. Both share a worldview that predates the splits of Eastern and Western Christianity and predates the Protestant Reformation that tore the church apart. Some in the church today want to restore the expression of faith and spirituality which is considered "traditional" to them but which in fact is a post-Reformation, largely nineteenth-century experience and appears today to be quite narrow in focus. Both Benedictine and Celtic traditions offer something richer, deeper, and more integrated, and I have found that each of these two traditions enriches the other.

My focus in these pages is "Celtic Christianity." This is not just a mental concept; it has been a lived reality. My questions in the museum haunted me: What happened to this culture? And how did the church that I associated with Irish Catholicism in my youth seem to reflect so little of that ancient church? I had to look at over two thousand years of history to get an adequate answer. Celtic Christianity is, of course, more than Irish Catholicism. My study discovered a church that was similar in Ireland, Scotland, Wales, and other areas of the northwest of Europe, including Northumbria and other parts of England itself. There was a great interchange of persons and practices in all these Celtic areas. I do not mean to imply that only the Irish formed the Celtic church nor that remnants of it could not be found elsewhere over the centuries. But I have emphasized the Irish experience both for economy and focus and also because of the availability of so many literary and archaeological remains. In addition, the Irish experience has directly influenced the Catholic Church in America, the largest American Christian church, and this was my starting point. Occasionally I refer to developments in other Celtic countries to remind myself and my readers of the larger Celtic reference.

My approach in this book is to follow a historical line to show the connectedness of the pre-Christian Celtic beliefs with the early Christian church of Celtic countries. Then I show how it changed, was subordinated and gave way to the larger Roman church, and yet how some of it endured. Finally I explore what it can offer us today as church and as individual spiritual seekers.

Though I cover aspects of history and culture, my focus is the spirituality of the people. Spirituality refers to the lived dimension of faith, how faith is lived out in everyday attitudes and behavior. It is not the same as creed, doctrine, or belief. There are many expressions of the one Christian, Trinitarian faith. Spirituality has to do with the soul and body in their expressions of love, with how the world is seen and appreciated, how one views humanity and its place in the cosmos. It is for this reason that this survey will consider various patterns of human living as indicative of a particular spiritual vision.

I write, therefore, as an Irish-American, a Roman Catholic priest, and a Benedictine monk. More basically, I am a human being, a spiritual seeker in touch with seekers who have gone before me and sharing with those who seek today. I believe Celtic Christianity has something to offer to anyone embarking on a spiritual journey today and is not confined to the Irish, Celts, Catholics, or monks.

Though I am, by practice, more in the Irish oral tradition as a teacher, I have responded to others' suggestions that I share some of this in writing. Bob Gormley, publisher of Orbis Books, attended one of my workshops and encouraged me to write. Still skeptical of my ability to do so, I was convinced by my friends Peg and John Gramling to write this book. In addition to Mairead Doherty I have been helped by Sandra DeRome, who has given me good feedback on my literary and stylistic writing, as well as some good reactions to the content. Robert Ellsberg, editor-in-chief at Orbis, has also given me much helpful criticism. I am grateful to all of them, as well as to Abbot Nicholas Morcone and my Benedictine community, who have supported me. May the Holy Three-in-One encompass all of them in love.

**Chapter
One**

Ancient Celts and Modern Christians

HE SEARCH FOR THE MEANING of Celtic spirituality
has led me back to uncover the culture and spiritu‑
ality of the ancient Celtic peoples. Many others share
my enthusiasm for these ancient peoples as well. The
various reasons for this awakened interest include the pursuit of
ethnic roots and fascination with pagan and new age connections.
A great deal more is now known about the Celts than has been
for centuries. Today the Celts are hailed as the first Europeans,
the earliest named people in Europe to whom we can look for
our roots. They are recognized as the "European Aborigines," like
Native American tribes already on the land with their own devel‑
oped culture prior to being conquered, driven out, or assimilated
by more powerful invaders.

My awakened realization of the presence and magnitude of
Celts in history emerged in many places. When I was a high school
boy in Latin class studying Caesar's Gallic Wars it never occurred
to me that the Celts in those books had any relationship to the

Irish, Scots, or Welsh. After all, the names of the Gallic chieftains Dumnorix and Vercingetorix hardly sound like O'Brien or McCarthy. But these Gauls were indeed Celts who were to be found across much of southern Europe until Rome forced them to move northward and westward. Later, on my first journey to Rome, I visited the Capitoline Museum of Antiquities. As I gazed on the marvelous statue of the Dying Gaul, I was awed by the dignity of this naked warrior without making any mental connection with things Celtic, nor did I realize that I was looking at a copy of a Greek sculptor's second-century B.C.E. picture of a Celtic warrior. In the same museum I also admired a wonderful sculpture on a first-century B.C.E. sarcophagus of battling Greeks and Galatians, the former in their customary uniforms, the latter naked but for a golden neck torque. Yes, these were the same Galatians that Paul would address in a letter a century later ("You senseless Galatians!"). And, yes, they were Celts. The names should have given it away. "Gaul," "Galatia," and "Gael" all come from the same root. I had not yet comprehended how widespread these Celts had been.

World history taught me that Rome and Greece represent for us the fonts of our Western civilization. Until recently we have relied heavily on writers of these two cultures for information about the Celts. The word itself, "Celt," is Greek, *Keltos*.[1] We are not certain what the word means. It is not the same as "barbarians" (*barbaroi*) but seems to mean something like "the other" or "stranger." The Celts never called themselves by that name but rather used various tribal names, such as the Belgi, Veneti, Senones, Carnutes, and so forth. The ancient Greek and Latin texts to which we look for data on the Celts include works by Plato, Pliny, Strabo, and Julius Caesar. Some of this literature, for example Caesar's *Gallic Wars*, was written for propaganda purposes and depicts the Celts as a fierce and worthy enemy, though inevitably inferior to the military and political prowess of Caesar and Rome.

My study also revealed that the records of Christian monks are a second source of Celtic history. Roman monks, such as Saint Jerome, struggled to rid themselves of their interest in the classical writings of Greek and Rome, considering all to be pagan and useless when faced with the gospel. But the Celtic monks relished the preservation of all history and literature and were not embarrassed to hand on the Celtic myths and legends. Some modern writers dismiss the writings of the Celtic monks too easily, believing that they did not respect the integrity of ancient stories. But the Celts had a unique way of seeing reality. They seemed to delight in telling the stories of Cuchulainn, Finn MacCumhaill and the Fianna, the poet Amergin, the goddess Bridget. We owe much to these monastic copyists whose sense of humor and respect for their sources are evident in the glosses, side comments, and illustrations in their renditions of the old stories. The most ancient legends of Ireland are preserved in a twelfth-century monastic manuscript entitled *The Book of the Conquest of Ireland*, more often referred to as *The Book of Invasions* (*Leabhar Gabhala*). It is suspected that the monks often changed ancient gods and goddesses into human superheroes, but they did little to cover up details of greed, sex, and violence. They surely were not ashamed of anything that was human.

I also found that an important aspect of this literature is the language in which it was written. The discipline of philology gives us tools to understand the culture, thought patterns, and beliefs of a people through their language. Nineteenth-century scholars, notably in Germany, found that the Celtic tongue belongs to the Indo-European family of languages and thus is a cousin of Latin-Italic, Balto-Slavic, Germanic, Hellenic, and other similar languages.[2] The Celtic language has two main branches, the Brythonic and the Gaedonic. The former probably came to Britain from Gaul and became embodied in Welsh, Cornish, and Breton. Clearly related to the Brythonic but differing in some respects are the Gaedonic languages of Irish, Scottish Gaelic, and Manx. The rudimentary Irish tongue was probably brought to Ireland by invading Gaels around 300 B.C.E. and later spread to Scotland and the Isle of Man. In Ireland the language went through four stages of development in its written form: Old Irish (600–900 C.E.), Middle Irish (900–1200), Early Modern Irish (1200–1650), and Modern Irish. Although it borrowed words from other tongues, such as Latin, Norse, and English, the Irish language is notable for its conservative tendency to preserve original forms and words.

Because of that slowness to change, we are able to reach back into the ancient mind with some ease. There is no evidence of any significant use of a written language in Ireland until after the arrival of the Christian evangelizers around the fifth century. Some of the earliest writings, such as Saint Patrick's *Confessio*, are in Latin, but an early vernacular literature soon blossomed, probably the oldest vernacular literature in Europe. Whether as oral or written, the language is central in understanding the Celtic culture and way of apprehending reality. The Celts have always been a people who delight in the power and value of the word!

Finally I found that the greatest development in our renewed appreciation of the Celts comes from contemporary scholarship in the field of archaeology. The combination of many new finds plus new methods for more accurate dating of old treasures is bringing forth a wealth of new knowledge. In 1846 at Hallstadt, site of ancient salt mines near Vienna in Austria, twenty-five hundred graves, dated between 700 and 500 B.C.E., were unearthed, producing the first tangible evidence of early Celts and their way of life. Soon after this, lake waters were drained at La Tène, Switzerland, revealing many more ancient Celtic artifacts. These findings precipitated the modern reappraisal of the Celts and a new interest in the study of their way of life. In 1978 in the city of Stuttgart on the Danube in Germany, the greatest twentieth-century finding was uncovered, the Hoffgott treasure, containing a funeral bier of a Celtic prince with a huge decorated cauldron, as well as other finds of bronze, wool, flowers, and horses, all dating to about 55 B.C.E. Then, in 1984, in Cheshire, England, a marsh was cleared for an airport runway, uncovering the twenty-three-hundred-year-old body of a young man evidently killed in a ritual sacrifice. He was first stunned by a blow to the head, then garroted with a twisted cord, and finally had his throat cut. The British Museum in London now exhibits his remains as "the Lindow Man." Other such findings have surfaced all over southern Europe. Many of these findings and their significance were heralded in the May 1993 issue of the *Smithsonian* magazine in an article entitled, "Once Maligned, Celts Are Now Touted as the First Europeans."[3]

I was beginning to find some answers to my first question asked at the museum: Who were these ancient peoples who developed such a sophisticated art and culture? Thanks to ancient classical and monastic sources, to language, and to archaeological break-throughs, we know a lot more about the ancient Celts than ever before. I began to feel that I might learn something from them for my own spiritual quest. Perhaps these ancient peoples might offer something special to the Christian church of today and to the modern world. So I had to discover more about just who these people were.

Origin and Ways of the Celts

I had expected to find evidence of the Celts in the British Isles but was surprised to find how much more widespread their domain actually had been. Their remains can be found in modern-day France, Belgium, southern Germany, Switzerland, Austria, Italy, Hungary, Slovenia, and Asia Minor. Their place of origin, how-ever, remains a mystery. Since they populated the river valleys of the Danube and the Rhine, some have posited their origin in the middle of Europe. Others believe they go back to the Black Sea area, and still others believe they originated in India or the Hi-malayas around 1500 B.C.E. The similarity of mythological stories and some anecdotal tales argue for the latter. Thus it is said, "If an Irishman would begin a story an Indian could finish it." I was fascinated to hear a musician friend confirm what I had already read, saying that he observed a similarity between Irish and East-ern music. Another musician told me that when he was learning to play the *bodhran* (Irish drum) he was surprised to learn how similar the rhythms of jigs, reels, and other Irish dance tunes were to Sufi music.

Britain was Celtic long before the Angles and Saxons invaded it in the fifth century C.E. and established the area we now know as England. The Romans helped to push the Celts back into Scot-land and Wales, but Celtic influence did not die out for some time in other areas of Britain such as Northumbria. Perhaps the Celts first came to Ireland from Gaul through Britain. *The Book of Invasions*, however, recounts the story of the Milesian invasion, Celts or "Gaels" coming to Ireland from northern Spain in the third or fourth century. Whether the previous inhabitants were also Celtic is a question still pondered. In any event the Celts became the predominant group in Ireland, eventually absorbing other ethnic groups that invaded the island through the subsequent centuries.

I don't remember encountering the Celts at all in world history and still don't see much about them in history books I pick up today. Lacking the centralization as well as the written documents of Greece and Rome, they were never taken seriously as a people of import. I believe we uncover a key to understanding the Celts when we realize they were never a unified empire. They were rather a fluid confederation of tribes united by language, religious outlook and practices, and the same lifestyles in war and peace. Their spread from east to west was due to their technological expertise in the iron culture of the day. For about one thousand years they spread across the continent. Their presence began to be felt from about 800 B.C.E., when they were noticed for their colorful costumes, use of horse and chariot, hunting, feasting, and war-making.

Though the culture may not have been the expression of a unified people, I nevertheless am immediately struck by its high degree of sophistication in art, technology, story, warfare, social mores, and religion. The recent archaeological finds have added to the wealth of what is known as "La Tène Art." Full of swirls, circles, and geometric figures, it is a form of abstract art unique for the time, especially in the West. These designs are playful, with a sense of the unending and eternal, showing some relation to or influence from the East.[4] Visually, the Celts liked color, brightness, movement, and human and animal shapes in abstract forms. I believe we are in touch with the Celtic mind and imagination with this characteristic of the "spiral knot." Their mind and their imagination differed from our modern scientific and literal way of seeing things. Theirs was more of a "symbolic consciousness" that reveled in images, symbols, myths. They saw reality from the lens of eternity, with no beginning or end, no distinction of the seen and unseen. The circle, rather than the straight line, emerges as the figure that expresses so much of Celtic life. The importance of relationships and kinship; all persons in the clan being on the same plane rather than in hierarchical positions; the equality of men and women, of king and peasant — such are characteristics of Celtic life that reflect this way of seeing reality.

But the Celts are probably known for their verbal skills even more than for their visual ones. Except for the Druids, or the Celtic spiritual and scientific leaders, who could communicate not only in their own Celtic tongues but in Greek and Latin alike, the Celts were generally an illiterate people. This may well have something to do with the phenomenon, noticeable in other early cultures and definitely found later among the Scots and Irish, that the spoken word cannot be frozen in written form or it will lose its life. The Celtic way of life had a profound respect for storytelling, poetry, and verbal jousting. The bard was an important person in the tribe. His task was to memorize thousands of lines of poetry to keep the traditions alive, as well as to compose new poems and songs to celebrate contemporary happenings. His sardonic "putdown" of a warrior was more devastating than a physical blow sustained in battle. So, too, warriors going into battle were accompanied by the bard proclaiming their genealogies and calling imprecations on the enemy.[5] Bards might be present at a birth to greet the new Celtic baby with the songs of the tribe. Feasts would center on dance, poetry, stories shared, and the singing of songs.

There is an ancient saying, attributed to the Irish, that says, "Never give a sword to a person who can't dance." A warrior who is not also a poet, an artist, or a musician cannot be trusted with a weapon — he will be a loose cannon! The Fianna (also called Fenians) were an ancient band of warriors whose special commission was to guard the high king of Ireland. They engaged in battles from May to November (from the feast of Beltaine, around May 1, to Samhain, around November 1) and then spent the winter resting, feasting, and engaging in poetry and music. Finn MacCumhaill, celebrated hero of Irish myth, became head of the Fianna. Finn had supposedly gained wisdom by burning his thumb on a grilled salmon and then sucking the thumb. He was renowned for his poems and stories. This quality of warrior-poet well describes many of the Christian monks too.

The gentle, poetic soul of the Celts was counterbalanced by the fierceness of their warfare. Always ready to quarrel and argue, they engaged in warfare primarily against other Celtic tribes for the sake of protecting, as well as increasing property, cattle, and other forms of wealth. Remembering the statue of "The Dying Gaul," I can picture the ferociousness of a primal strike of Celts. Their hair is spiked back with lime, their bodies are naked except for a gold torque around the neck and perhaps a belt around the waist for sword or dagger. With a mighty yell they come over a hill surprising and striking terror in a foe. It must have been quite a sight, and the hope was that the enemy would turn and flee. Unfortunately the Celts were not always certain about what to do next! Julius Caesar learned how to wear them down and defeat them. Sword play, chariots and horses, and chain armor were all used to successful advantage, much of this imitated by the Romans. The belief that the soul was to be found in the head led to head-hunting and decapitation in battle. A victorious warrior would carry the head of a defeated foe on his belt or place it on a pole.[6] And yet a sense of fair play, the forerunner of medieval chivalry, also characterized the Celts in battle. A battle of clans could be settled by a representative warrior from each group engaged in hand-to-hand combat. Examples of this practice can be found in the stories of the great hero Cuchulainn.

The Celts did make war on other peoples as well as on each other. They sacked Rome in 387 B.C.E. and were in a position to dominate history. As it turned out, that distinction went to the Romans. In 225, following some important victories, the Celts suffered a major defeat at Telemon north of Rome. By 200 the Romans were again in control of all of Italy, and by 100 they were moving into Celtic Gaul. Julius Caesar conducted his Gallic warfare between 58 and 50 B.C.E. where, by his own account, he ruthlessly killed 1,192,000 Celts. A temporary unification of the Celtic tribes occurred under Vercingetorix, but Caesar outmaneuvered them and brought about the Romanization of Gaul. Rome looked down on many Celtic customs, such as human sacrifice. But it is noted that Caesar brought Vercingetorix, the defeated organizer and leader of the united Gallic revolt, to Rome, publicly humiliated him, and had him slowly strangled to death. Soon afterward, in 43 C.E., Rome invaded Britain, and the Celts were driven back to the northern and westernmost extremes of Europe.

On the domestic level, the degree of Celtic civilization was evidenced in the development of horseshoes, handsaws, chisels, files, seamless iron rims for wheels, iron-tipped plows, and the rotation and fertilization of crops. On the personal level, the Celts were a vain people; they used soap and body oils to keep clean, bathed in milk, and wore jewelry, rings, torques, necklaces, and brooches. The hair was considered to be a special sign of beauty, and much attention was given to it. Men shaved chin and cheeks but cultivated great mustaches. They also wore breeches as well as cloaks, a practice imitated by the Romans, who then began to wear trousers while riding horses.

The tribe or clan was the principal social unit of Celtic society. One's identity came from belonging to this tribe, and loyalty to it was paramount. Many clans formed a *tuath*, a people. Each group had its own king (*Ri*), and there were provincial kings and a high king (*Ard Ri*). This was not a hereditary position. The king was chosen by the clan under the direction of the Druids. The king had to embody what was the finest in the clan and had to be whole physically. He occupied a place not so much above the people as at their center, not so much in a hierarchical position as in a unifying one. The king might share his quarters and sleep with a whole group of the clan.[7] This image of kingship strikes me as an example of intimate relationship, even in an authority figure. It helps me to see how fealty was easily transferred to Christ and to understand the intimate relationship that was felt with him as king.

Although the men held most positions of authority and honor, women too had many rights in Celtic society, particularly when compared to Roman and Greek societies. Women could hold property and keep their dowry after being married. They could initiate divorce. They also engaged in warfare. The teacher of warrior skills for Cuchulainn was a woman on the Isle of Skye. Queen Medb

(Maeve) of Connacht is a central protagonist in the epic *Tain Bo Cualnge* (The Cattle Raid of Cooley). A woman named Boudicca (Boadicea) led the Celtic insurrection against the Roman invasion of Britain in the first century. Some challenge the interpretation of the place of women in Celtic society and believe we are too much influenced by our contemporary way of seeing things in imputing rights to women. A recent study by Peter Berresford Ellis, a Celtic scholar, argues, however, for the reality of women enjoying many positions and rights among the Celts.[8]

I find this background relevant to our study of Celtic spirituality, for many of the old ways were absorbed into what would be the Celtic Christian church. But we see the connection most clearly when we look at religion in Celtic society. There is no doubt that the Celts were a very religious people. They had an intense belief in the afterlife, a daily awareness that the other world was very close to them, and they perceived some coming and going between this world and the other. This belief contributed to their indifference to pain and death. It also gives us some insight into their attitude toward ritual human sacrifice, which was practiced among the continental Celts and in Britain, and possibly in Ireland as well. Their image of the afterlife was probably that of a better version of this life with rich and sensual experiences. One vision of this experience was *Tir na nOg*, the land of eternal youth to be found far away under the western sea.

They also believed that this other life impinged on and interacted with the present life. Spirits of ancestors and fairies were to be found in various places, particularly in those identified as "thin spaces," or at "thin times." Deaths and wakes were such times and occasions. A particular thin time was the annual feast of Samhain (around November 1) when the space between the old year and new year allowed spirits to move more freely in the world. Don't we see remnants of this in the Irish wake and our American holiday of Halloween when we imagine spirits and ghosts on the loose? I also find a remnant of this attitude toward time and place in modern Irish life. In telling a story an Irish person places much emphasis on where something happened (place is important), but not when (time is not). Still another way this can be observed is in the Irish sense of time. The Irish seem more like a Mediterranean people at times and not like other northern peoples, who treasure punctuality.[9] A pub may advertise live music at 9:00 p.m. but don't be surprised if the musicians don't show up much before 10:00!

Integral to an awareness of the other life was the Celtic propensity to find the divine in all of created nature. Whether the Celts were animists, believing a tree or a flower actually embodied the divine, or whether they saw the divine as intimately reflected in all creation is not very clear. Much of what we know of Celtic gods and goddesses comes through Roman writers who often interpreted the Celts' religion through their own understanding of the divinities. All sorts of beliefs and superstitions were surely part of Celtic life as well. But, most importantly, there was tremendous admiration for, respect for, and love of nature. The earth and all its creatures was a source of beauty to delight in, accepted as good, celebrated in its seasons. The dark side of nature was also acknowledged, and means of protection were sought in order to live with that reality as well. Incantations against dark forces were common in Celtic life. Later the Christians would pray a form of protection prayer called a *Lorica*, or Breastplate, and Saint Patrick is credited with one of these prayers.

Celtic art and poetry mirror the hallowed place of the created material world in the Celtic vision of reality. As with all primitive agricultural peoples, the earth was reverenced as the source of fertility and life. Sacred groves, rather than any building, were the places for worship and sacrifice. The oak tree, in particular, in its stature and strength, was the sign of the divine and its setting the site for religious ceremonies. Saint Columcille (Columba) would later come from Derry, which means place of the Oak. Saint Bridget is associated with Kildare, meaning Church of the Oak.

Tending to tradition, leading the clan in sacrifice, and guiding the communal decisions were the Druids. These mystery figures of the Celts have often been regarded as their priests, but they were more a combination of philosopher, theologian, lawyer, judge, ambassador, scientist, and counselor. Caesar wrote that these people trained for twenty years or more before being acknowledged as full Druids. They were the "magi," the astrologers of their people, reading the signs of nature and the heavens to advise the best time for making war or planting crops. They united the culture inasmuch as the Druids of the various tribes met with each other and deliberated with each other. There is good reason to believe that there were female as well as male Druids.

The Druids were able to read and write and were aware of civilizations beyond their own. They taught in riddles, especially liking triads, thus handing down the myths and values of the people. The Celts love for style and eloquence would find its perfect fulfillment in a verbal duel in which two Druids would rouse each other to a point of emoting a tribal prophecy.

The Druids supervised the annual feasts and solemnities. These rituals unified the culture in a way that political initiatives could not. They led prayers before battle but did not engage in battle themselves. They also presided at most marriage, divorce, and funeral rites, particularly at the death of a king or warrior. Funerals were occasions for games and celebration with much dancing, singing, and phallic mimes that joined death and reproduction. In summary, the Druids were at the center of Celtic life, providing a structured office to embody the spiritual, mystical, earthly, and cultural values of a people otherwise united only by language and origin. In Christian times, we see how easily the Celts saw the monk as the continuation of the druidic figure. The image was explicitly used by Saint Columcille when he proudly professed that Christ was his Druid!

This summary sketch of the ancient Celts, truly a fascinating people, gives us a background for understanding the origin of some characteristics of Celtic Christianity and of modern Celtic consciousness as well.

Are There Any Modern Celts Today?

And where would one find such a modern Celtic consciousness? I certainly was not aware of any such reality in my Irish-American Catholic upbringing. Of course many people claim Celtic ancestry, sometimes the more so as they are distanced from it in time and space. Culturally, the reality of being Celt has been connected to the question of language. It is the language which enfleshes the spirit of a culture. This is true for any people but is especially significant for Celts, who were a people of song, poetry, and story-telling. There are no completely Celtic-speaking peoples in the world today. Does that mean that the living link with the Celts has been broken and that only a museum or tourist interest remains? I do not believe that is so. After years of decline and neglect, an intense interest in Celtic roots and identity sprang up in the nine-teenth century. Myths, stories, poems, songs, and prayers of the Celtic tradition were revived. Contact was made with the pockets of peoples, particularly in Scotland, Wales, and Ireland, where the language and Celtic way of life was still thriving. The ensuing rise of nationalism, in various degrees in each country, has led to a further reclaiming of the older ways.

In 1961 the Celtic League was formed in Wales to improve re-lations among the six modern Celtic nations of Alba (Scotland), Eire (Ireland), Mannin (Isle of Man), Cymru (Wales), Kernow (Cornwall), and Breizh (Brittany). Its goals are cultural, linguistic, economic, and political.[10] The league is concerned that the origi-nal languages have all but disappeared in Cornwall and on the Isle of Man. Brittany however does show a slightly increased use of old Breton. There is a "Gaelic Renaissance" taking place in some parts of Scotland, where the Celtic roots have managed to survive in the outer Hebrides and the Scottish Highlands. In Wales, on the other hand, a Celtic language is spoken by a larger percentage per capita than anywhere else in the world.[11]

In addition to these "six nations," there are other peoples and places that claim some Celtic origin or culture. The northern prov-ince of Galicia in Spain (site of the famous medieval pilgrimage center of Compostela) expresses its Celtic roots in its music, song, and dance.[12] There are still those in present-day England who claim a Celtic heritage. This includes many Anglicans who be-lieve their church to be in the Celtic tradition. In France, outside the specifically Celtic area of Brittany, there are those who claim a Celtic past. This was seen in the reinstating of Vercingetorix as a national hero, honored as a symbol of resistance to outside aggression. A monumental statue in his honor can be seen in Alesia, the area of his last holdout against the Romans. In France there is also the popular cartoon character "Asterix," who battles against the Roman invaders in the setting of ancient Gaul. Finally we note that the language and culture has also endured in the New Breton area of Nova Scotia in Canada.

While all these sources are helpful in determining how the ancient Celtic culture and its expression endured to the Christian era, it is especially to Ireland that we must turn for an in-depth look at Celtic Christian spirituality. Although Roman invasions were responsible for pushing Celts back from center stage in Gaul and Great Britain, the fact that the Romans never carried out their planned invasion of Ireland became quite significant. Ireland developed as a rural, townless society well into the late Middle Ages and the old Celtic ways survived. Historical traces of this culture and spirituality are more apparent in Ireland than elsewhere. For instance, the La Tène art of the ancient Celts continued to appear for a long while in Irish Christian art, such as the Book of Kells, sculptured crosses, and other artistic expressions. The Anglicization of Britain affected Scotland and Wales more than Ireland, bringing the Christian churches there under the authority of the archbishop of Canterbury. This is not to deny that aspects of the Celtic spirit continued to thrive in those countries, but they did not do so with the same autonomy as in Ireland. Today Ireland remains the largest Celtic nation, and the only one that is politically free and independent. The Isle of Man gained some independence from England and has its own Parliament but is still not totally autonomous. In contemporary Scotland there is now the expectation of a restoration of its own Parliament and the obtaining of some regional self-government within the United Kingdom. By a narrower vote of the people, the Welsh have decided for the erection of a National Assembly with some limited powers of local government but also still subject to the power of Westminster.

The Irish Christian experience is largely responsible for the way the Catholic Church developed in the United States, Canada, and Australia, where so many of the first immigrant clergy (and especially the bishops) were Irish. In my consideration of Celtic

Cross-inscribed stone at Gallarus Oratory (eighth century), Co. Kerry.

Christianity, therefore, I shall be looking principally at Ireland, its history, its church, its struggles to survive, and its present-day Celtic heritage.

The Celtic Tradition and the Christian Church

Before exploring Celtic Christianity, it might be helpful to review the underlying themes, movements, and characteristics that come from the ancient Celts to the Christian church. I like to call them "fault-lines," for they are like underground seismic lines that are liable to surface and become manifest at unexpected times. These are enduring traits which, to me, identify the Celtic personality still alive and influential today.

First, the Celts were an intensely verbal people who lived in an acutely oral culture. Poetry, proclamations, music, and story were warp and woof of daily existence. Druids and bards were among the most respected people in this society. Similarly monks, priests, musicians, poets, teachers, and storytellers were central figures in Celtic Christianity.

Second, a corollary of this verbal nature of the ancient Celtic people was their imaginative way of seeing, hearing, touching, and feeling reality. There was a peculiar non-linear way of apprehending time and space so that past and present intertwine; those who had died were still present, and the other world was transparent in the everyday ordinary ways of life. It was a mystical view of reality and would lead to wonderful prayer forms in the Christian era. It would likewise influence art, architecture, writing, and decorating. How easily, with this worldview, would the Celts take to the Christian doctrine of the communion of saints. You can hear them saying, "Of course we are close to, and related to, all our ancestors and the saints who have gone on before us. They are fellow companions with us on our journey."

Third, we see that the social unit of the Celts was the clan, the tribe. This is a localized group and only loosely connected to other clans and tribes. This proved to be both a strength and a weakness. As a strength it led to local responsibility for the self-development of the people and the emergence of local authority, the choosing of the king and the discerning of who qualified as Druid or bard. This also contributed to a strong communal sense in the Celtic church. The weakness was the fighting and raiding between clans, constant in-fighting, and the inability to unite for a common purpose or against a common enemy. Sadly, this weakness has appeared recurrently down through history and endures today.

A fourth characteristic of these people was their great respect for heroes and warriors. Cuchulainn and the Red Branch of Ulster, Finn MacCumhaill, Oisin, the Fianna warriors, and many others were the subjects of many of their songs and their memory was a source of strength when embarking on new battles. There was a fierceness and passion in the fighting of their wars. Their adulation of heroes was easily applied and transferred to Christ and the saints. The warrior spirit was channeled into an intense and passionate spirituality that insisted on penance and heroism. Both men and women were heroes and warriors in line with the generally equal place of women in Celtic society, and this attitude continued in the Celtic Christian church. The warrior spirit was balanced by the gentleness of the poet and mystic. And paradox was also a feature of Celtic spirituality: never a black-and-white "either-or" attitude but more a "both-and" embracing of opposites.

Fifth, the mystical bent of the Celt was especially evident in the great love of creation and of all nature. This was not merely a romantic view of creation but a healthy respect for it, recognizing the dark side, the menace of nature's mighty powers as well as its beauty. This love of nature is central to Celtic Christianity and is the source of a wonderful heritage of nature poetry.

Finally, among these Celtic fault-lines I single out the Celtic tendency to wander, to roam, to explore. Voyage stories are part of the Celtic lore handed down to us. And voyage, as well as pilgrimage and search, are characteristic features of Celtic Christianity.

There are, no doubt, other aspects of the Celtic culture that can be traced in the development of the Celtic Christian church. These six, however, are chosen with the hope of raising initial awareness of the spiritual aspects of the Celtic church.

Chapter
Two

Christianity
Comes to the Celts

I CONTINUE TO FIND the ancient Celts a most fascinating people, one that speaks to many of our contemporary concerns. One of these concerns is finding an expression of our Christian faith which creatively responds to the prevailing hunger and thirst for spirituality and meaning in life. As I look to the early experience of the Christian church in Ireland and the other Celtic countries, I become even more fascinated. There is something refreshing about it all that strikes a chord in my soul and says that this is something good and right. The Celts quickly, easily, and thoroughly embraced the Christian faith. It spoke to their soul. The same Trinitarian, Christ-centered, sacramental church built on the scriptures and the teachings of the apostles that was spreading over Europe, Asia Minor, and northern Africa came to these most remote areas on the north and west of the known world. But among the Celts this church developed in some unique ways.

The first thing I notice about the Celtic church is that it came into being very peacefully. In other areas of Christian evangelization there was resistance to the point of rejection and persecution of the new way. "The blood of martyrs is the seed of Christianity" became a well-known maxim. But martyrdom is practically unknown in the Celtic church, although some martyrdom did occur in Britain. There are specific references to the martyrs Aaron and Julius in the middle of the third century in the area of Gwent in southeast Wales. There is absolutely no evidence of martyrs in Ireland before Queen Elizabeth I in the late sixteenth century. No, Christianity was a peaceful and almost natural development in Ireland.

In recent Christian history, the doctrine of the threefold God has largely become an abstract and theoretical doctrine, a "mystery" that you embrace as a sign of your Christian commitment, kind of a secret code that identifies you. The Jesuit theologian Karl Rahner decried the fact that the Trinity has become a rather irrelevant doctrine to most Christians. He wryly observed that if the church were to declare a change in this doctrine and say there were two or four persons in God, it would make no difference to most Christians — just something to accept on faith. Since Rahner wrote this some thirty years ago, we have begun to rediscover the Trinity as central to our faith. Made in the image of God, we find it to be good news to learn that this is a God of relationship, of love, of intimacy, of everlasting sharing, giving, and receiving. That God should be a threefold God was one of the theological and psychological insights of the early church.

To the Celts, who already thought in terms of threes, this must have seemed very natural. They had already thought of their pagan deities in symbolic and abstract images. The phenomenon of "shape-shifting,"[1] common to gods and heroes alike, meant that a god or hero might appear under various aspects. That one might also be many could be imagined. The threeness was explicit in images such as the goddess Bridget, who appeared in three forms: the goddesses of fire, of poetry, and of fertility, all three named Bridget! This Trinitarian consciousness permeated Celtic spirituality. An awareness of the threefold God shaped prayer after prayer, and a triad way of expressing prayer became common as well. One such ritual prayer was a practice immediately following the birth of a child. The baby was carried in a circle around the room three times in the direction of the sun. Then it was handed over a fire three times in purification, and finally three drops of water were placed on its head. Thus was the child marked with the Trinity prior to its formal baptism.

A second "natural" propensity of the Celts for Christianity was their way of looking at the world and all reality. I have already focused on their openness to the other world in the immediate material world around them, their seeing the sacred in the ordinariness of creation. I have also described what I called their "symbolic consciousness," an ability to see more than what is immediately visible. I believe this was a natural opening to the sacramental worldview that Christianity proclaimed. God could be touched, felt, tasted in bread, wine, and oil, and in human word and touch as well. How natural indeed! Isn't this what we present-day Christians have been trying to revive since the Second Vatican Council? The centuries leading up to that council had seen a "spiritualizing" of the sacraments and of creation in general. Theology stressed the philosophical "substance and accidents" of sacraments, their validity and liceity. Bread no longer looked or tasted like bread but was etherealized into an air-like wafer. The cup and wine disappeared despite the fact that Christ told us to celebrate Eucharist in that mode. A few drops of water sufficed at baptism, a smudge of oil for anointing. Were we afraid of matter? Was there a relationship here to our shame about the body, and even a downplaying of marriage? And doesn't the Celtic perspective seem much healthier as well as much more theologically correct for us today?

The Celts, a people of the word, took to the Word of God, embraced the scriptures, and soon applied their great artistic skills to the preservation of the Bible as well as other classical texts. A people who loved heroes embraced Christ and the saints as their new heroes. With little difficulty the old Celtic gods and heroes were subsumed into Christian saints. Lugh, one of the favorite Irish gods, a sun god known for the splendor of his countenance, was soon recognized in the mighty figure of the archangel Michael. Shrines to this favored warrior angel were soon to be found on mountain heights of Cornwall, Brittany, and the island monastery of Skellig Michael. As elsewhere, Mary, the mother of God, became an important feminine expression of God's love for the people.

The Celtic Church and Rome

The Celtic church developed in its own unique way, absorbing much of its pagan antecedent. The relation of this church to Rome and the larger universal church emerges as an issue, especially for those who see the Celtic church as something distinct from the church of Rome. I find that this relation is sometimes reduced to a simplistic black-white, good guys-bad guys scenario. I do not believe the Celtic love of paradox and mystery, of unity in multiplicity substantiates such an approach. Neither do the facts of history. On the continent many Celts had embraced much of Roman culture without much resistance after Roman imperialism had spread its way northward. The relation of Celt to Roman was not always adversarial. As far as the Roman church was concerned, the Celts accepted its reality as the communal expression of the faith and embraced being part of the one Catholic Church.

There is no doubt, however, that the Celtic church then developed in a distinct way. The Celtic church in most of Britain would give way to both the new Anglo-Saxon culture and the church customs brought by Saint Augustine and the missionaries sent by Pope Gregory from Rome. Scotland and Wales, however, remained too remote for either of these influences to have their full effect. Celtic enclaves in these two areas of Britain remained Celtic. But, most significantly, the planned Roman invasion of Ireland never took place at all. The Irish were never part of the Roman empire nor exposed to its day-to-day ways. On the continent, the church spread with the empire and took on many of its organizational attributes. The system of dioceses with bishops as overseers was developed along with the urban spread of the empire, a diocese being set up in each urban setting. As the empire crumbled the church organization was often the only way to keep things together, and bishops emerged as administrators, stewards of people's needs, slowly acquiring a base of power and authority. The bishop of Rome was the exemplar of this development. But in Ireland, and largely in Scotland and Wales as well, there were no urban centers. Bishops and priests there did not acquire such power bases. The base there was communal, and abbots and abbesses emerged as leaders. The model was not hierarchical as the Roman one was, but more communitarian and relational. Women continued, at least in the earlier years, to have positions of authority and leadership and enjoyed equal rights. There is evidence, for instance, of groups of deaconesses called *Conhospitae,* who had a liturgical role in the Eucharist.

Some of the theological problems that beset Rome never impinged on the Celtic church. Saint Augustine, for an example, had come from a sect called the Manichaeans. This group held a dualistic view of reality, believing in a cosmic split of light and darkness. Material beings, including the human body and sexuality took on the aura of evil. There has been a recurring tendency to this belief in Christianity. It emerged earlier among Gnostics and would emerge again later in Albigensianism and Jansenism. This mindset never entered the Celtic Christian church (though it would affect Irish Catholicism at a much later date). The Celtic belief in the goodness of creation and all material being was too strong for this.

To sum up, I believe that the Celtic church had a freedom of expression in its history that led to practices unlike those of the Roman church; nevertheless it never believed it was not part of that church. It was a local church that was in communion with all other local churches forming the universal church with the bishop of Rome, who enjoyed a special ministry of primacy. Now that is exactly what the Second Vatican Council talked about in reaffirming the understanding of the local church. The trend since the Middle Ages was to see the church as one monolithic unity organized so that dioceses and parishes were lower divisions of the one church. The council reestablished the ancient view of local churches in communion. Bishops were once again understood to govern their dioceses in their own names as part of a college of bishops enjoying unity with each other and with the bishop of Rome. Now, after many years, this doctrine of the local church is fraught with much tension and not yet fully accepted. Since the time of the dissolution of the Roman empire, the Roman church has tended to respond to any centrifugal forces by stressing the need for unity through centralization. The Roman Curia has demonstrated a paternalistic attitude, attempting to protect other churches from harming themselves through error. The grassroots voices that ask for a hearing and sometimes for change are dismissed with the statement that the church is not a democracy. What is not faced is that the church is not imperialistic Rome, or feudal Europe, or a Byzantine court, or a medieval monarchy either. But the church has been, and sometimes still is, all of these. The church must be incarnated in human forms. The Celtic church is an intriguing example of another way it once was so incarnated. Could it not offer an alternative as a local church to a bureaucratic, power-based church today?

Non-Roman Influences on the Celtic Church

Under the influence of Augustine the theology of the West concentrated more and more on issues of sin and grace. Thanks to Tertullian Western theology had already begun to become more legal in nature. The Celtic church did not get embroiled in the same issues. This early church was influenced significantly by the Eastern Christian churches of Asia Minor. Through trade there were even direct contacts with the East. Knowledge of the churches of both Jerusalem and Constantinople was widespread. The way of the early desert monks was emulated in Ireland, where the desert figures of Saints Paul and Anthony would be found on many high crosses showing the special devotion they enjoyed. As indicated earlier, the Celts already shared some cultural affinity with the East in music and myth.

The Christian faith primarily came to Britain from Gaul and then from Britain to Ireland. Surprisingly we find that there were a number of Eastern cults flourishing in Gaul at the end of the first century.[2] The names of the earliest Christians in Gaul appear to be Greek and Oriental. The first bishop of Lyons, presumably the main Christian center in Gaul, was Pothinus (87–177). He came from Asia Minor, as did Saint Irenaeus of Smyrna (130–200), who succeeded him as bishop from 178 through the year 200. Irenaeus was a significant person in early Christian theology. He had been a protégé of Saint Polycarp, himself a disciple of John the Evangelist. The Johannine influence seems evident in Irenaeus and, it is suggested, through him to the Celtic church.[3] Irenaeus lamented that he was in exile among the Celts, but his own theology of wholeness and his respect for the goodness of creation was in harmony with the Celtic worldview.[4]

Another connection to the East came through John Cassian (360–435). Possibly born somewhere in the area of the Baltic, John entered a monastery in Bethlehem and later lived the monastic life in Egypt. From this firsthand experience of Eastern monasticism, he came to Marseilles in Gaul, where he founded two monasteries about the year 415. His writings on the monastic and ascetical life had a large impact in the West, including the influencing of the Rule of Saint Benedict (480–560) in Italy, soon to dominate Europe. John Cassian also influenced the development of monasticism among the Celts. Monasticism would soon in fact become a major aspect of the Celtic church.

A Church of Place

I grew up in an urban part of New York. Our attached "town house" had a small backyard and an even smaller lawn area in the front. My earliest years were stable and simple. But when the Second World War ended, I became part of a society that was ever more mobile and changing; it was a time of technological explosion bringing new and better things for all. Yet my love of nature, of open space, and my desire to find unity with all of creation has only increased since then. In the Celtic attitude to both God and creation I have found a path to a healthy spirituality. The Celts have bequeathed to me a sense of the sacred of the land and the sacredness of place.

The importance of the land in Ireland and one's attachment to it has lasted into modern times. Irish farmers have personalized their relationship to land and called their fields by names. The owning of one's own land was a key factor in the tragedy of the Cromwellian persecutions, the penal laws, and the great famine, as well as later struggles in Ireland. *The Field*, a film with Richard Harris shown in our theaters in the late 1980s, was a sad portrayal of a tragedy surrounding a man's losing his field, and in that struggle losing his son as well.

The earlier reference to "thin places" pointed out that some places in particular were boundary points between the material world and the other world. Celtic Christians had a sense of living on the edges, the margins, of pressing themselves to the limits to find such places. Some would seek their "place of resurrection," which they discerned to be a particular doorway to heaven, the place where they hoped to die and thus to rise. The poetry that we find among later monks expresses this sense of place in the image of the natural world as a doorway to the sacred.[5]

Some places were considered to be more naturally sacred by their very essence. Islands were such places. Caldey off Wales, Iona off Scotland, Lindisfarne off Northumbria in Britain, Inishmurray off Sligo, Inishmor off Galway, and Skellig Michael off Kerry in Ireland were all such sacred places. Mountainous high places were other naturally sacred places. In addition to the high shrines to Michael already mentioned, there is Croagh Patrick, the holy mountain of Patrick in Mayo, and Mount Brandon, the site of Saint Brendan's hermitage on the Dingle Peninsula. I have stood on some of these sacred places and have sensed the immanent presence of God. Of course there is also the sea, the ever-present sea, surrounding these island peoples. It affected their vision, their art, their poetry, their sense of impermanence in this life.

Cemeteries, *raths*, or ring forts, and mounds in a field (not to be touched), wells which join the underworld and the upper world and bring forth life — these are still more examples of Celtic sacred places. Being exposed to a sacred place could also be a fearful and awesome encounter. Prayers of praise were common but prayers of protection from the dark side of the unknown were also part of this spirituality. A common ritual practice was that of the *caim.* Celts would draw a circle in the earth around themselves with a finger as they prayed to the Trinity to encircle and protect them.

While some places were naturally sacred, others became so because of their historical connections. Bangor in northern Ireland is an example of a druidic college that became a monastery attracting thousands of students. Before the arrival of Christian monks, Iona was a pagan religious center known as Innis na Druineach, the Isle of the Druids. Already mentioned was Saint Bridget's center of Kildare, the Church of the Oak, presumably also a former druidic place of worship. Then there is a whole mythology associated with Glastonbury in Somersetshire in the southeast of England near Bath. Legend associates this place with the earliest Christian foundation in Britain, a first-century church linked in myth to Joseph of Arimathea. It would become the site of a Celtic monastery and its "tor" (high craggy hill) crowned with still another shrine to the archangel Michael. By the eighth or ninth century Glastonbury was a Benedictine monastery, which flourished until Henry VIII suppressed it in 1539 and put to death its last abbot, Richard Whiting. Stories of Saint Patrick and King Arthur are associated with Glastonbury.

But even earlier than Christian times, Glastonbury was a Celtic druidic site. Its identification as the Isle of Avalon, the City of the Dead, adds to this significance. Today the large remains of the abbey with the grave of Arthur and the Glastonbury Tor are part of a museum park and place of pilgrimage. It is also a site revered by many new age adherents who ascribe astrological significance to Glastonbury as the center of British pagan religious mysteries. In ancient times the tor, known as the holy mountain of Gwynn ap Nudd, was thought to be the entrance to the underworld.

A Church of People

The Celtic Christian church was a church of people, of heroes and charismatic figures. It emphasized community, relationships, the equal gifts of all whether man or woman, cleric, lay, or monk. I see a number of people as particularly significant in the early development of the Celtic Christian tradition. They are all called "saint" but none was canonized, for such a formal process did not yet exist. They were simply acclaimed by the people as their local heroes. Many of their names are unfamiliar to American readers today. The Celts had a whole army of saints celebrated in various places. We have become accustomed to think of accepted Celtic names such as Patrick, Michael, Mary, and Bridget, as well as names of apostles such as Sean/John and Seamus/James in the naming of children. The nineteenth-century Catholic Church borrowed names from the continent that had no Celtic tradition — Ignatius, Alphonse, Aloysius, Catherine. Today we hear more of the older names again — Kevin, Colum, Aidan, Enda, Diarmuid, Nuala, Naebh. When I last stayed at an Irish Bed and Breakfast with a young family, I met their four children, all under ten: Darragh, Cathal, Ciara, and Orleigh.

One Celtic saint whom I had known little about was the man who was to become the patron of Wales, Saint David, or Dewi (520–89). He was a monk in the monastery founded by Saint Illtyd, disciple of John Cassian. David became the head of a monastery near his birthplace in Pembrokeshire. Here he became famous as preacher and evangelizer. The present cathedral of Saint David's was begun in the twelfth century, after the Norman invasion, and is now a national shrine. The austerity of David's monastic regimen included a sparse diet in which vegetables, especially wild leeks, were common.[6] His name is connected with about twelve other monasteries, including Glastonbury, where he built a church.

The main source for our knowledge of David comes from the eleventh-century biography, written in Latin, by Rhygyfarch, himself a monk of Saint David's, based on ancient material as well as considerable legend. One such legend is the story that Patrick, who might have been a Welshman himself, had intended to preach to his countrymen. An angel, however, appeared to Patrick and directed him to Ireland, saying another had been chosen for Wales. This story is wonderfully commemorated in the 1989 oratorio *Dewi Sant* by the Welsh composer Arwel Hughes.[7]

Our God hath not disposed this place for thee,
But for a son not yet delivered, nor be born until thirty years
    are past
Be not sad, be joyful, Patrick, giv'n to thee em'rald isle across
    the sea,
And to these people thou shalt be Saint, apostle of Christ:
    God hath ordained.

The story goes on to have the mother of David, Non, come to the church to hear Gildas prophesy about her unborn child:

O maid, the son thou shalt deliver
O'er Cymry's saints shall be the ruler,
To reign supreme till judgment day,
Though poor his way, yet full of grace and power and dignity
    and honor.

And, further on, praise is given to David:

And in Vallis Rosina the Sainty David built his Holy House.
And there he laboured and bore his witness, custodian of the
    Faith;
A prince o'er the saints of this island,
A help to the needy and a friend to the lonely,
A father to the faithful, a terror to all heretics;
His gentle correction, and deeds of compassion.
O Prince of the Faith, O Prince of the Faith.

Other heroes of the Welsh church included Samson (485–565) and Gildas (500–570), who was the author of a diatribe on the laxity and corruption of the church in Britain. Much of our knowledge of church life in these areas in the sixth century comes from his writings. Early heroes of Scotland include Saint Kentigern (518–603), known as Saint Mungo, the dear one. He was the founder of Glasgow, at whose cathedral his body is still venerated. Other Scottish saintly people included Saint Serf, known as the Apostle to the Fifes, and Saint Modan, Apostle to Stirling and Dumbarton. Saint Conan brought Christianity from Scotland to the Isle of Man. Saint Adomnan was the ninth abbot of Iona and biographer of Columcille.

Our list of early Celtic heroes is incomplete until we look at Patrick, primary patron of Ireland. Saint Patrick is accredited as the great Apostle to the Irish, though other missionaries from Britain or Gaul had apparently preceded him there, and there is some indication of Christians on the southeast coast of Ireland by the year 400. The first factual reference to this is of Pope Celestine sending Bishop Palladius to Ireland in 431. The generally accepted date for the birth of Patrick is 387, and his coming to Ireland as bishop in 432.

The breakdown of the Roman empire meant a loosening of its control in Britain. Irish pirates began to patrol the west coast going from Wales up past Cumbria in northern England to Scotland. Somewhere along that coast lived the family of the youth Patrick. He was not quite the age of sixteen when he was kidnapped and brought to Ireland as a slave. Patrick then was forced to take care of a man's herds, which he did for six years. I believe this experience was a pivotal and significant one for Patrick. I can certainly commiserate with him and wonder how I would deal with such a happening in my life. I am a healthy young man who suddenly loses his freedom, his home and family, his schooling. I am terribly lonely and homesick as I spend time by myself "in forests and on mountains" watching animals. I am underfed and underclothed "through snow, through frost, through rain," and so am "humiliated by hunger and nakedness, even daily." I am on the edge of the known world, surrounded by a strange pagan people. I feel abandoned and perhaps punished by God for my past sins.

Adversity makes or breaks all of us. I do not know what Patrick's experience would have done to me. It is clear what it did for Patrick. Solitude and suffering were a desert experience that purified his soul and made him aware of the intimate, providential presence of a loving God who really cared for him. So he could write:

Then the Lord made me aware of my unbelief, so that — however late — I might recollect my offenses and turn with all my heart to the Lord my God. It was He who took heed of my insignificance. Who pitied my youth and ignorance, Who watched over me before I knew Him and before I came to understand the difference between good and evil, and Who protected and comforted me as a father would his son.[8]

From then on Patrick's faith was molded by the elements of God's creation and by the Spirit whom he learned to hear in his own heart. His six-year servitude ended when he heeded the voice in a dream directing him to escape and to begin a two-hundred-mile trek to a ship that would take him home. But the story did not end there. The sailors obviously held him as a captive, and he spent four weeks with them after the sea journey traversing what appears to be western France. Again he escaped to begin a new segment of his life's story. Patrick returned to his parents in Britain, but his was not to be a life of domestic ease. Again a voice in a vision came, this time identified as a man named Victorinus coming from Ireland with a letter containing the "Voice of the Irish." Patrick heard the voice "from beside the western sea" crying out, "We appeal to you, holy servant boy, to come and walk among us." Another voice, which Patrick identified as coming from the Spirit, continued to direct him back to Ireland. We do not know the details of what education he finally received, nor how and where he was ordained priest and bishop. But return to Ireland to preach the gospel to the pagans of the country he surely did.

There are two later seventh-century sources for our knowledge about Patrick. Bishop Tirechán left his *Account of Patrick's Journey* and Muirchú wrote his *Life of Patrick*. These accounts stress his episcopal position, his struggles against Celtic paganism, his journeys across Ireland, his great work of evangelization and conversions obtained, and his role as a wonder worker. These are in the form of traditional medieval hagiography, which takes historical facts and embellishes them with images that place the protagonist in the shadow of other great saintly figures. In the case of Patrick, the stories include his lighting of the fire on Slane in defiance of the local king, his casting out the snakes from Ireland, other miracles, and his teaching on the Trinity with the shamrock. The historical accuracy of facts such as names, places, and dates of these two documents is not taken very seriously.

To gain a deeper knowledge and appreciation of Patrick, I have been using the writings of Patrick himself in his *Confessio*, an autobiographical account written later in his life when he was under attack from various critics. There is also his *Letter to Coroticus*, in which Patrick protested the captivity of some Irish chieftains taken by Welsh raiders. These writings are clearly authentic, and they reveal a very appealing person, someone helpful today as a role model of response to God's love coming even in adversity. The writings are dominated by a strong faith in the Triune God, a mark which would become characteristic of the Celts. They are enmeshed in the scriptures, revealing a profound knowledge of the Bible. Many scriptural quotes are simply entwined in his sentences as he recalled them without explicitly quoting them. The Epistle to the Romans is one of the books of the Bible he quotes most often.

The *Confessio* is the portrait of a very simple, sincere, and humble man. He was treated harshly by his own ecclesiastical peers. One confidant betrayed him by making public a sin Patrick had committed before the age of fifteen, a person in whom Patrick had confided in a spirit of penance at a later time.[9] The *Confessio* also reveals Patrick defending himself against accusations of an illegitimate ministry in Ireland, of taking money for his ministry, and of wasting his time on such a remote and marginalized people. Patrick came to love this very people who had enslaved him, even though he was chained and imprisoned at least once more as a bishop. He was undaunted in energy, baptizing thousands, ordaining many priests, and caring for the poor. His letter to Coroticus reveals a singularly brave and outspoken voice against slavery, an institution as yet still accepted by the church in Rome. It is true that he shared the growing Roman admiration for virginity as an especially holy state, but this did not undermine his respect for marriage and women. In one passage he simply comments that he baptized one "most beautiful as a grown woman." He thought of himself as rustic and unlearned, and yet the modern study of his writings is revealing of a much greater degree of sophistication than hitherto realized. His voice is a unique one in sixth-century Celtic Christian history, and we have nothing with which to compare it.

Patrick's faith and trust are beautifully summed up in this statement:

> I take this to be a measure of my faith in the Trinity that, without regard to danger, I make known God's gift and the eternal comfort He provides: that I spread God's name everywhere dutifully and without fear, so that after my death I may leave a legacy to so many thousands of people — my brothers [and sisters], and sons [and daughters] whom I have baptized in the Lord.[10]

Patrick tells us that he has thrown himself "into the hands of Almighty God," and he ends his testament by writing:

> I implore those God-fearing believers who agree to read or accept this document which the unlettered sinner Patrick composed in Ireland, that none of them will attribute to an ignorant person like me any little thing I may have done, or any guidance I may have given according to God's will. Consider, and let it be truly believed, that it may have been rather the gift of God. And that is what I have to say before I die.[11]

Patrick, in his own words, remains for me the archetypal Celtic Christian. He is penitential and ascetic. He engages in continuous and repetitive prayer. He is ever more and more passionately in love with God. He loves sacred scripture. He is close to the God of nature. He has a rich, poetic imagination with the openness to hear God in vision and dream. He thus remains a powerful symbol for the beginning of the Celtic church in Ireland. I find it unfortunate that some would revise history today and cast Patrick into the role of Roman colonialist. Later church writers and leaders might have changed him into such a figure, but his own writings tell the story of a man remarkable for his time — and our time as well.

Chapter Three

Celtic Monasticism

HE CELTIC CHURCH, much like the Eastern Orthodox Church, had a profound respect for monks. More basically, these early Christians believed everyone was called to holiness and not just to salvation. All were enjoined to live the life of a monk, even if married with children. The Christian life had to be a life of prayer and renunciation for all. This was a strength of the Celtic church but also, at times, its weakness.

Monasticism can be a very dangerous thing. And monks, whether of the male or female variety, can be very troublesome people! First of all, monks can stir people up to give themselves wholeheartedly and fully in a passionate commitment to God. The search for God becomes everything and anything that gets in the way must be jettisoned. One must not be encumbered in the spiritual journey but must travel light! The monk is single-minded[1] and determined in his or her search for the divine, the transcendent, for that which is both beyond and within all life and all things. This impulse has also led some to speak of a "monastic archetype," that is, an image in every person's soul that prompts one to go on an ultimate quest for the beyond. Some enflesh this quest in a monastic lifestyle and in a monastery environment to support them in this single-minded quest.

There were no monks in the Old Testament, but the prophets often served a monastic function and brought their vision to bear on the institution of the monarchy. Prophet and king, sometimes in tension with each other, were part of the unfolding story of God's revelation to His people. Prophets were still around in New Testament times, as evidenced in some of the Epistles. The Christian monastic movement, however, developed in Syria, Palestine, and Egypt as Christians sought some more focused and totally absorbing form of life to be able to follow Christ. This happened especially with the end of the persecution of Christians when the age of the martyrs was no more. Martyrs were thought to be the really perfect Christians. Now that they were no more, how could Christians keep their spirit alive? Thus the monastic search of anchorites (hermits) and cenobites (community fellows) came about. In time they would often be "dangerous" for the church, annoying both clerical and lay folk by their example of full-hearted commitment and sometimes demanding reform of the church, beginning with clergy.

However, there has also always been a second way that monasticism can be dangerous. It has been dangerous, in a mild sense, when it has become too institutionalized. At times it has been swallowed up in clericalism. It loses its force and flavor. Then it just helps to support the status quo and even reinforces mediocrity. This has happened when monks have been successful, accepted, and especially when, by their buildings and lifestyle, they have become comfortable and secure. Monastic structures and institutions have even impeded the human maturing of some monks who never had to confront the real issues of life.

A still more serious way that monks can be dangerous is when they become self-righteous in their holiness, too esoteric and cut off from the simple and human, perhaps even fanatical. Tendencies to excessive penance and to the shunning of the opposite sex as equated with a virtuous turning away from evil are two examples of this dangerous dark side.

I believe that Celtic monasticism, as well as other forms of monasticism such as the Benedictine tradition, has been dangerous in both the positive and negative ways I have described. I have been holding up the positive aspect of Celtic Christianity for our understanding as well as our emulation. But not everything in the past is to be embraced and repeated. The appreciation of the good side is in fact enhanced by seeing the dark side, the aberrations of the good. By doing this we can truly learn from the past. The Celtic church was a wonderful monastic church. But, at times, it became soft and tepid and in need of reform. And at times it became too rigid and severe.

Introduction of Monasticism to the Celts

The Celts in Ireland and Wales, as well as in Scotland, quickly embraced monasticism. The fact that it happened so swiftly is as difficult to explain as the rapid acceptance of Christianity itself. Because of the scarcity of documents apart from the writings of Patrick, we cannot say for sure when the first Christian monks came to Ireland and Wales, nor if monasticism had reached Ireland before Patrick. It is possible that Patrick himself was exposed to monasticism while in France.[2] On the other hand, if Patrick had actually established the traditional Roman structures of church such as diocese and parish, as some claim, then something soon occurred after his death to change the Celtic church into a monastic church. The surest thing that can be said is that monasticism soon colored the Celtic way of Christianity.

Monasticism appealed to a warrior people who were attracted to an ascetic lifestyle. It appealed to a mystical people who had relied on Druids to interpret the signs of the cosmos. It appealed to a tribal people who lived closely in community. It appealed to a marginalized people who saw the monk as one who lived on the edge of things, on the very margins of life. It appealed to a people who saw in pilgrimage and the spiritual journey the sense of adventure and quest that their ancestors had enjoyed. All these appeals coalesced in the emergence of Christian communities based on monasticism. Religion was not just an adjunct to one's regular life; it had to be an integral part of life. And it had to be embraced in a fully committed way. The early Celtic Christians, similar to the monks of the eastern desert, looked for an alternative to shedding one's blood as a total embracing of Christian discipleship. Thus it was that a "green martyrdom" arose in distinction to the known "red martyrdom." The green variety referred to a life of fierce asceticism and penance. It was a way to follow and identify with the high king, Jesus, in his passion and death. Another expression of this commitment brought about the term "white martyrdom," which referred to going into voluntary exile. For a people attached to their land and their native country, this was seen as a way of following Christ in his "self-emptying."[3] Just as Christ let go of his divinity to fully embrace humanity, so the monk would let go of his beloved land to follow Christ.

The words "monk" and "monastery" conjure up all sorts of images for us. Most come from medieval monasticism, and some are very romantic and stereotypical. You should not, however, picture a large medieval stone monastery, a huge church, and a quadrangle cloister in its midst when you imagine a Celtic monastery. No, the latter was more a "monastic village" than a huge complex of buildings. The village had a stone wall around it to keep animals in and thieves out. Within the walls were many small huts, whether wooden buildings or crude structures of mud and wattle. Later, especially in the west of Ireland, stone buildings were erected. Many remains of stone *clochans*, called "beehive huts" in English, are scattered over the countryside of Kerry. Some common buildings such as small oratories were part of the enclosure. These monastic villages were the closest social reality to towns that existed. They were the centers of religion but also of commerce, trade, agriculture, recreation, and education. Paradoxically they were often built "on the edge," that is, in remote places, but at the same time seemed to be accessible and near crossroads of trade routes.

It is the human dimension of such villages that particularly fascinates me. These "monks" included men and women, priests and lay persons, and even a bishop or two as part of the community. The old Celtic forts had men and women living in respective men's and women's houses, except for the married, and this system continued. An abbot or abbess was the administrative leader of the community, leaving the sacramental and evangelical functions to bishop and priest. The latter would both serve the community and also go outside to preach Christianity to clans who had not yet accepted Christianity. There is no indication that any large church buildings were ever built, and it is probable that the Eucharist and communal acts of worship continued to be celebrated outdoors as had formerly been done in oak groves. The natural connection to God's creation was continued in the new Christian rites.

Celtic monasticism differed from its Eastern predecessors in two regards. First, the Celts were much more open to people and more evangelistic in their approach to the society in which they lived. Second, they were much more open to study and the intellectual pursuit of learning. In these new monastic villages, within one generation a people who had been illiterate became the copyists and writers in monastic scriptoria, the monks who preserved the great learning of the Irish past, its stories, poems, and prayers. Other cultures are also indebted to these scribes of Ireland. The Irish monasteries were responsible for the preservation of much of ancient civilization, Roman and Greek included.[4] In time the educational centers at these monasteries attracted students not only from all over Ireland but thousands from Britain and the continent as well. In addition, the elaborate art of the ancient Celts was kept alive and perpetuated in the illumination of manuscripts and the design of metal work such as chalices and crosiers, as well as brooches and jewelry.

Organized monasticism in Ireland began with Saint Enda (c. 460–530). He himself had been a monk at Saint Ninian's monastery Candida Casa at Whithorn in Scotland. Ninian (360–432) is the first truly historical figure we can find on the monastic scene of these isles. Returning from Rome, Ninian encountered Saint Martin of Tours (c. 316–97), who had founded a monastery at Liguge in Gaul before becoming bishop of Tours. Martin is credited with bringing monasticism to the West. Jean Markale, a historian of Celtic civilizations, claims that we touch the purely Celtic aspects of Christianity in Martin. At Tours this saint established a church that had a great influence in western Gaul, the area of the country least colonized by the Romans.[5]

Apart from the possibility of direct contacts with Eastern monks, we can thus trace the point of arrival of monasticism in Ireland (and probably Wales too) from Martin in France through Ninian in Scotland. According to one story, Saint Patrick spent time at Ninian's monastery studying the history and customs of monastic life. We do know that Enda returned to his native Ireland in 484 to found a monastery at Killeeny on Inishmor, the largest of the Aran Islands. Today this is the site of the remains of a small church in a graveyard filled with many ancient unmarked graves. Here on a clear day Galway is visible across the bay and the two smaller Aran islands and the Cliffs of Moher appear in the distance. Also on Inishmor are the remains of a chapel dedicated to Saint Ciaran, who studied under Enda before founding his own monastery at Clonmacnois on the eastern shores of the Shannon River, some eleven miles south of modern Athlone. The monastic settlement of Clonmacnois exemplifies the paradox of many Celtic monasteries: it was both remote and accessible. Clonmacnois was situated near the crossroads of a route travelers would use going east to west, and it became a great monastic center of art and learning. Today there are many fine stone remains to be found, churches, graves, and also three wonderful high crosses, which are now in a modern visitors center.

Ciaran is reputed to have been mentored by another early Irish monastic founder, Saint Finnian of Clonnard (died c. 549). Finnian spent time as a monk in Gaul and wanted to go to Rome when an angel supposedly advised him that whatever he could find in Rome could be found in Ireland, where he should go to renew the faith and belief following in the path of Patrick. Finnian has been called the Patriarch of Irish Monasticism and Teacher of the Saints. It is said that he tutored three thousand saints, twelve of whom were recognized as "the Apostles of Ireland," including Columcille of Iona, Ciaran of Clonmacnois, and Brendan the Navigator of Clonfert. Finnian founded a number of monasteries in

Burial remains at monastic settlement of "Teampall Brecan" on Inishmor, Aran Islands, about seventh century.

Statue of the "Pilgrim" at remains of St. Ciaran's Monastery, Clonmacnois.

Ireland, among which Clonnard on the Boyne River in Meath was preeminent.

Glendalough in the Wicklow Mountains is another great monastic site of the early Irish church. I spent five days there and enjoyed the beauty of the glen with its two lakes, the mountains, and the many ruins. Here Saint Kevin, who had been a soul friend of Ciaran, spent time as a hermit and then founded a monastic community. His small cave on the side of a precipice twenty feet above the lake was difficult to get to but, as I discovered, the experience of this dramatic sight was well worth the effort. Kevin must have been a character in his own way. Stories tell of his having kept women at bay. But other stories tell of his softness and sensitivity to nature. A recent poem by Seamus Heaney is one of the many renditions of the story of Kevin befriending a blackbird making a nest in his hand while he prayed. Kevin's small monastic site grew in many stages over the years and became a great center of holiness and education. Kevin died in 618, but Glendalough continued to flourish for centuries.

Another monk whose story especially appeals to me is Saint Colman of Kilmacduagh. After some time as a solitary on the Burren in County Clare he founded a monastery there and was also bishop of the area. Legend says that, while a solitary, he was attended by a cock who would wake him, a mouse who would keep him awake, and a fly to mark his page and line in the psalter as he prayed. Such are the wonderful little stories of the relation of monks to nature that we so often come upon. Colman's Well remains a site of popular devotion on the Burren near the extensive ruins of the twelfth-century Cistercian Corcomroe Abbey. In the spirit of Colman, two very friendly dogs walked with us as we climbed the Burren hill to find the well and there to drink and pray.

Celtic Monastic Women

The Celtic church, true to its pagan roots, was not exclusively male in its leadership and spiritual teaching. A very important figure is

The author at the remains of monastic city at Glendalough (St. Kevin's Monastery) in the Wicklow Mountains, Co. Wicklow.

Saint Bridget (452–524), second only to Saint Patrick as a patron of Ireland and a personage receiving great honor and devotion. The figure of Bridget is part history, part mystery. Known as "Mary of the Gaels," she may be seen as one who in her very person demonstrates a definitive feature of the Celtic Christian church, that is, its ability to be thoroughly inculturated into the local scene, in this case by assimilating many of the pagan Celtic antecedents. Prior to the Christian era, there was a goddess named Bridget, a goddess of fertility, a goddess who was visaged as maiden, mother, and crone. She was connected with poetry, healing, and hearth. The stories of Saint Bridget are difficult to separate from the stories of the goddess Bridget. The Christian saint was the daughter of a Christian slave woman and a Druid master and the two strains combine in her to create her mystique. She was an independent woman who gave away the belongings and wealth of her father, who in exasperation finally allowed her to become a nun. Bridget founded the double monastery of Kildare, where she served as abbess until her death. Nuns at her monastery kept an eternal flame burning there, a custom said to have originated with female Druids residing at that spot in olden days. The flame endured until it was extinguished at the time of the Reformation. It has recently been relit by the Sisters of Saint Bridget in Kildare, who have revived her cult and lead pilgrimages to the well of Bridget located outside the town.[6]

A reminder that this assimilation of ancient pagan worship into Celtic Christianity perdures was voiced by Father Colm Kilcoyne, an Irish priest from Cong in County Mayo, when he wrote:

> I love the Irish Catholic Church — when it is left alone. I love it when it is a way of life, not a political weapon. It is at its most honest when it is part pagan, part Christian, part Celtic beliefs, whatever you are having yourself. The Irish Catholic Church is at its worst when it tries to play politics. It is too free, too contradictory, too tolerant, too wild a spirit to be a political power.[7]

Saint Bridget was certainly a historical person, and the importance of Kildare for many centuries testifies to the foundation, around the year 500, of a major church, an episcopal see but one under female governance. We depend on later sources for our knowledge about her. In the seventh century the earliest life of an Irish saint in existence was written — the *Life of Bridget* by the monk Cogitosus of Kildare. This life, hardly historical, weaves together earlier legends with stories of the nun Bridget. Cogitosus portrayed Bridget as the head of a dual monastery with a bishop as her coadjutor. From this writing we have portrayals of Bridget as the midwife to Mary at the birth of Jesus. She was also pictured as the one who helped Mary and Joseph find Jesus when he was lost in the temple at the age of twelve. The fact that these events took place some four centuries earlier does not seem to have bothered people who had a mystical vision of time and space quite different from our own.

Other stories of Bridget in this *Life of Bridget* tell of miracles, particularly with regard to supplying food and drink in the time of need. Sometimes the need was considerably less acute, as when she turned water into beer! She hung her cloak on a sunbeam, replaced stolen sheep, transplanted a tree when it could not be moved by workmen. Cogitosus ends his story of Bridget's fame with these words:

> Who could convey in words the supreme beauty of her church and the countless wonders of her city.... "City" is the right word for it: that so many people are living there justifies the title. It is a great metropolis, within whose outskirts — which St. Bridgid marked out with a clearly defined boundary — no earthly adversary is feared, nor any incursion of enemies. For the city is the safest place of refuge among all the towns of the whole land of the Irish with all their fugitives.... And who could number the varied crowds and countless people who gather in from all territories? Some come for the abundance of festivals; others come to watch the crowds go by, others come with great gifts to the celebration of the birth into heaven of St. Bridgid who, on the First of February, falling asleep, safely laid down the burden of her flesh and followed the Lamb of God into the heavenly mansions.[8]

There are two later lives of Bridget which are even less reliable for historicity than that of Cogitosus. One of these sources tells the story of her being consecrated as a bishop, albeit mistakenly, by Bishop Mel. Whether this story is true or not, Saint Bridget is much revered today for her example of the positive role of women in leadership. She also was a firm advocate of the necessity of having what the Celts called "soul friends." This term referred to an intimate spiritual friendship which involved the exercise of spiritual direction and mentorship in a mutual relationship of trust and love. Many of the Celtic saints traveled great distances to meet others whom they regarded as their soul friends. Bridget is quoted as having said that anyone without a soul friend is like a body without a head.

Second only to Bridget as a popular female saint is Ita (Ite or Ide) of Kileedy, originally called Deidre, who died around 570. An abbess, Ita founded a monastery, possibly for both women and men, in County Limerick at Kileedy. There she conducted a school for young boys, which Saint Brendan attended. Ita has been referred to as the Foster-Mother of the Saints of Erin. She was also famed as a powerful confessor, gentle and compassionate, but one who gave tough penances. Her grave at Kileedy is in the ruins of a Romanesque church where her monastery formerly stood. The ongoing devotion to her is evidenced by the flowers frequently found at her grave. Nearby there is a famous holy well, almost invisible now, where for centuries children were brought to be cured of smallpox and other diseases.

Other female monastics whose lives are remembered in writing include Saint Darerca and Saint Ibar. The lack of more detail about the early women monastics is regrettable and probably indicates the later neglect of history to remember the place of women. I do recall, while cycling over Inishmor, finding a roadside sign pointing back into a field to the remains of a small early church with bowed walls. It was dedicated to Surnaidhe, an unknown woman saint. That church in its setting struck me as a metaphor for the many women in church history who have gone unnamed and forgotten in men's accounts. The interesting fact, though, is that the earliest known Irish monastic foundations had women as their heads. It may be conjectured, therefore, that this monastic movement was pioneered by women. Virginity had developed, at least partly, as a way for women to be able to find independence from male domination. Both in the eastern desert and in Ireland it seems that female monasticism developed very quickly and perhaps prior to the movement among men.[9]

Monks as Pilgrims on a Journey

Brendan the Navigator (486–578) was born near Tralee in western Ireland and is honored as the patron of Kerry. Tutored by Saints Ita and Finnian, he is said to have spent some time in both Wales and Scotland before settling as a hermit on the top of Mount Brandon, the second highest peak in Ireland. This mountain, rising directly from the sea for 3127 feet, towers over the adjacent areas and is often shrouded in mist. Here Brendan must have looked out at the open sea.[10] Flowing down from the mountain and into the sea is Brandon Creek. Its harbor is supposed to be the place from which Brendan went forth on his sea voyages.[11] At this point legend takes over from history. The ninth-century tale of his journeys, the *Navigatio,* describes his fantastic explorations. The text of this tale survives in 120 manuscripts and is the basis of the legend of his trip to North America. This delightful book became immensely popular in medieval times. One charming episode is about the Easter Mass celebrated on a small island in the ocean. At the end of Mass the island moved and Brendan and his companions discovered they had been on the back of a whale.

In 559 Brendan founded a monastery at Clonfert in County Galway. A cathedral later was built on the site and still exhibits a wonderful twelfth-century Romanesque doorway with carved heads of many saints, including Brendan. Tradition says that this was the burial place of Brendan. Next to the present cathedral, keeping alive the monastic heritage of Brendan, is a lay community called the Emmanuel House of Prayer.

Brendan was an adventurer, willing to take risks and to explore the unknown. This Celtic propensity to wander, to roam, to go on pilgrimage was not so much a missionary or evangelistic undertaking but rather a means to follow Christ. Other monks adopted this practice in various ways. Going off to sea in a *curach* (small boat), setting oneself adrift without oars and letting the wind determine one's destination was an expression of this wandering and self-abandonment that characterized "white martyrdom." Brendan's story, the *Navigatio,* served as an example of this impulse to wander and identified life as a spiritual journey. The *Navigatio* is a spiritual odyssey, similar to those of the Greek *Ulysses,* the Latin *Aeneid,* and the later Arthurian stories of the search for the Grail. It is an archetype of the call many of us still hear today to leave all and follow Christ, to take the narrow road, to set out and not look back, to risk losing our life so we may find it.

Still another expression of the monastic impulse, indicative of both search and penance, was the desire to push to one's limit, to place oneself physically out as far as one could go in trust of the caring God. This tendency is exemplified in the remoteness of some monastic sites and is particularly visible in the choice of Skellig Michael, an island easily identified by a huge double peak of rock soaring upward out of the sea some seven miles off the Kerry coast from Valencia. Under the patronage of Michael the Archangel, this place would certainly need an angel's protection in a storm! The wonderful monastic remains still found at Skellig Michael date back to the sixth century, and the name of Saint Finan is associated with its foundation. Monks inhabited this wild refuge for five centuries through the Viking invasions, and the last historical evidence of monks inhabiting the site comes from the eleventh century.[12]

Since 1992 the modern Skelligs Experience Visitor Center in Valencia introduces people to the unique history, folklore, and wildlife of the Skelligs, both the smaller Skellig with its mammoth population of gannets and other birds, and the larger one, Skellig Michael, with its monastic remains. I was fortunate enough, with the weather permitting, to get a ride out to the island with a boatman from the village of Portmagee. He left our little group off at this wondrous site and allowed us a few hours to climb and explore it. Here we beheld six corbelled beehive huts, two

Beehive huts, standing rock figure, remains of a seventh-century monastery on top of Skellig Michael, an island eight miles off the coast of Co. Kerry.

boat-shaped oratories, stone crosses, slabs, and graves, plus a later, medieval church. We gazed on the remains of the terraced garden where monks grew their food. Standing on this height I called to mind the words of Jacob in the book of Genesis (28:17), "How awesome is this place! This is none other than the house of God, and this is the gate of heaven." Indeed the site, the views, the feeling of this place was awesome. It far exceeded many better-known shrines I have visited throughout the Christian world. An interpretative guide helped us to appreciate the site. He gave some background and mentioned that these monks were considered to be very important and essential to the people on the mainland. Monks at prayer and penance were appreciated as a significant part of the social fabric. This is an important insight to a vision where the sacred and secular were intertwined and spiritual realities were part of mundane, everyday life. I would like to hope my life as a monk would be considered as helpful and fruitful to Christian people today as the lives of the monks of Skellig were back then.

Columcille: The Warrior Monk

The Celtic church was a church of heroes, of charismatic leaders, of strong and passionate men and women. The old Celtic warrior spirit was alive in them, now put to the service of the gospel and the following of Christ, the high king. Today I find it hard to iden-tify many warrior Christians. We have tended to emphasize the passive aspects of spirituality: obedience, loyalty, submission. I like to think that the active virtues of courage, strength, outspoken-ness, decisiveness, and the ability to stand up for something are good Christian virtues as well. I see these virtues in Columcille, son of royalty born in Donegal in 521. His name means "Dove of the Church," and he is at times known simply as Columba, or Dove. But he was also called the Wolf, and I suspect he was al-ways a wolf in dove's clothing. He was a warrior, but one who could dance — for he was also a poet, writer, and storyteller.

Columcille had a heart afire with the love of God and the love of Ireland. He founded a number of monasteries, including those at Derry, Durrow, and Kells (all three of which had groves of oak trees, sacred to the Druids, growing on their original sites). The story is told that he secretly copied a psalter which Finnian of Moville had brought back from Rome. Once discovered, he was condemned for this breach of copyright, but he did not give up easily and simply returned the manuscript. Tribal warfare followed, in which a number were killed in the battle of Culdreimhne.

Whether because of a punishment inflicted by a synod or a self-imposed penalty, Columcille joined the line of wandering monks and went into exile. In 563 Columcille, now forty-two years old, departed from Ireland along with twelve other disciples. He set out in a spirit of adventure for the Irish kingdom of Dal Riata in Alba (Scotland). Yet there was sadness in leaving the beautiful homeland behind, a sadness he would often feel in his later life. His poignant farewell to Ireland is captured in a poem, written later but attributed to him.

> Pleasant indeed this hill of Howth
> high over the white-breaking sea
> proud hill of the many ships,
> vine-growing, eager, warlike peak.
>
> Peak where Fionn and the Fianna stood,
> that once boasted the riches of kings,
> where brave Diarmuid brought
> Grainne one day, in bold flight.
>
> Most beautiful peak of all Ireland
> lording high over a sea of gulls;
> leaving it a heartbreaking step,
> radiant peak of the ancients.
>
> Great the speed of my curragh
> its stern towards Derry,
> penance for me to travel by sea
> to Scotland's edge.
>
> There is a grey eye
> which will look back upon Erin,

> never will it see again
> the men of Ireland or her women.[13]

Columcille was determined to travel until he could no longer see Ireland. At his first stop he looked back and could still see the blessed isle. So he went on until he landed on the isle of Iona, an ancient sacred site, where he established a monastery that would become a center of religious life for the entire Celtic world. The writings of Adomnan, Columcille's biographer and himself the ninth abbot of Iona, help us to grasp the picture of the early years of this settlement. The monastery flourished, and monks remained there through the ninth and tenth centuries despite the ravages of Viking invasions. The island was revitalized in 1203 by the establishment of a Benedictine monastery, which remained until its dissolution in the sixteenth-century Protestant Reformation. Pilgrims continued to visit the ruins, and the isle was recognized as a sacred and truly "thin place."

Columcille's warrior spirit now found new challenge as he set out to evangelize the native Picts, proceeding on his way through Scotland, Britain, and Saxonland. He went head on with many native leaders to call them to faith and belief in his beloved Druid, Christ. His monks were involved in preaching, baptizing, founding churches and monasteries, and choosing leaders of the new Christian church which was taking root there. Columcille became known for many healings, miracles, and the taming of wild beasts, including the Loch Ness Monster. He shared the typical Celtic love of nature, sitting for hours on his favorite rock and gazing at the sea. On June 9, 597, fourteen hundred years ago, Columcille died in the monastery chapel after asking his brothers to carry his body there in the middle of the night. For three days and three nights a violent windstorm blew, not to cease until Columcille was interred; then the sea and air once again became beautiful and calm.

Pilgrims like myself today visit this sacred spot hallowed by Columcille and his monks and remember the mystique of this warrior monk, disciple of the great hero, Christ. In 1874 the duke of Arygll inaugurated a program of preservation. The cathedral church of the Benedictine abbey was restored between 1899 and 1910 for worship. In 1938 the Rev. Dr. George MacLeod founded the Iona Community, a living ecumenical community that continues to this day. Once again pilgrims come to this place of mystery, see the wonderful old crosses, and pray at the site where Columcille landed on the shore, at the abbey, and at other places on the isle associated with this Celtic mission.

Columban: Feisty Monk Evangelizer

The final major Irish monastic figure I want to look at is also the one with the most historical and verifiable factual basis. I admire him also as a distinct and strong personality, another warrior monk. Columban, born in Leinster in 543, was a prolific writer and left many traces all over Europe. In Ireland he first studied under Sinell, a disciple of Finnian of Clonnard. He then embraced the monastic life at Bangor in County Down. Here he became learned in theology and was the chief lecturer in the monastic school. In this monastery by the sea he would watch the ships coming from and going to Scotland and elsewhere. After thirty years there, the call to be a pilgrim came to him. With the usual twelve disciples he set out for Gaul. Thus began a great trek across the continent. With him the Irish monks were on the move with a great sense of mission. The historical significance of this mission is summed up by the Irish Carmelite Peter O'Dwyer in this way:

> In the centuries of the barbarian invasions and conquests, Ireland contributed two special gifts to Europe. One was high moral seriousness, the acceptance of God's law and of the gospel counsels, and the putting of these into effect without compromise. The other was the emphasis on the cultivation of the mind. Columbanus is the only sixth-century Irish saint who has left us a collection of writings which enable us to determine the character of saintliness of the Irish church in early medieval times.[14]

In Gaul, Columban first established monasteries in Burgundy at Annegray, in Luxeuil, and in Fontaines. These three monasteries in turn would found fifty-three other new communities in the ensuing years. Writing in Latin, Columban composed two monastic Rules, the Regula Monachorum and the Regula Coenobialis. He was also an outspoken preacher and attacked the local clergy, royalty, and lay people for their lack of morals. He was known for his championing of minority causes and for his tolerance of people who were different or marginal. His Celtic spirit shone in a fierce asceticism and independent disposition that brought him respect but also involved him in controversy wherever he went. Soon asked to leave Gaul, he went on to Switzerland and Austria. In some sort of disagreement, Columban left his disciple, Gall, in Switzerland, who himself then laid the base for the great monastery of Saint Gallen. Later in life Columban sought reconciliation with Gall. At the time, though, he moved on to found a monastery at Bregenz in Austria and probably others as well. Finally he crossed the Alps into Italy and settled at still another new monastic foundation at Bobbio near Milan. He obviously made an impression wherever he went, for many places are named after him across Europe.

In addition to his monastic writings, Columban has left a penitential, six letters, thirteen sermons, and some poems. The "penitential" was in the line of a new genre of Irish writings which consisted of lists of appropriate penalties for sins committed. As time went on, these tended to become more and more severe. The penitential was also part of a private confessional system, possibly an outgrowth of the soul friend relationship, that developed in Ireland and would contribute to the private form of the sacrament of penance throughout the Roman church.[15]

Meanwhile these new monasteries on the continent became involved in preserving much of classical antiquity as well as early Christian writings. At a time when Europe was experiencing a "Dark Age," this often meant the rediscovery of ancient sources that had been lost in the overrunning of monasteries and urban centers by barbarian incursions. The life and writings of Pope Gregory the Great (pope from 590 to 604) attest to his efforts to alleviate the material and spiritual needs of a depleted civilization. In one of Columban's extant letters, written to Gregory in 600, he expressed his admiration for the pope and his pastoral sensitivities. Here was someone that Columban admired and tried to emulate in his own strident way. Another letter, written to Pope Boniface IV in 613, was another matter, being quite critical of the pope for not upholding the decisions of the Council of Chalcedon (451). Here are some excerpts:

> ...I am sad that the See of St. Peter is touched by scandal. I know that the business is above me and that I must seem to be placing my face among the hot coals. But what is my face to me — my public face, my reputation, — when it is zeal for the faith that must be made public?...We Irish who live at the edge of the world, we are pupils of Saints Peter and Paul and of all the disciples — who were inspired by the Holy Spirit to write the divinely inspired scriptures....Our possession of the Catholic faith is unshaken: we hold it, just as it has been handed on to us by you, the successors of the holy apostles. This assurance makes me strong and spurs me to urge you to resist those who revile you, who proclaim that you tolerate heretics, and call you schismatics....So just as your honour is great because of the dignity of your See, you must take great care not to loose your honour through some untowardness. For you will retain power openly as long as you follow right reason. For he is the sure keeper of the keys of heaven who through true knowledge opens to the worthy and closes to the unworthy.[16]

There is no indication that Columban received any response from Rome, but the letter does bring out another aspect of the Celtic church. It has already been shown that Columban embodied the monastic, ascetic, and penitential spirit of the Celts. He was also a pilgrim who sought solitude but perchance became a missionary. He was on the side of the oppressed and involved in what we would call issues of social justice. But his letter to Rome also shows that he was Catholic, one who was a faithful member of the body of Christ, which he saw as the one church under the pope of Rome. There is no question that the Celtic church was not part of the church of Rome. It was not a separate church but one that recognized its own legitimate local customs. The authority of the pope was recognized. On the other hand, this writing is not a subservient and purely passive approach to this legitimate authority. Like other medieval saints after him (such as Bernard of Clairvaux and Catherine of Siena) he felt it was his duty, in love and in fidelity, to admonish and counsel the pope. This is far different from the later attitude that would characterize the Irish church in its submissive loyalty to Rome.

Columban died in 614, but other Irish monks continued this monastic and missionary advance into Europe. Saint Kilian (died 689) settled in Wurzburg and is honored as the patron of that German city. In that same country, other Irish monasteries appeared in Trier, Mainz, and Cologne. Monasteries were founded by Irish monks in Austria at Vienna and Salzburg, in Switzerland at Reichenau and Berne, in Italy at Milan, Verona, Fiesole, Lucca, and Taranto in the south, and many other places on the continent. Meanwhile there was movement in the opposite direction as well. The Venerable Bede, in his *Ecclesiastical History*, wrote that numerous people came from England and the continent to study at the monasteries in Ireland.

The Monastic Inheritance

This monastic and missionary advance was the apogee of the Celtic Christian church. This was a church based on the monastic spirit. Heroic and passionate men and women were following their hero, Jesus, through penance, asceticism, solitude, and pilgrimage that was intended as an exile in honor of Christ but that brought forth rich missionary and evangelical fruits. This was a church characterized by a gentle way of life and yet found in austere monastic settlements and island retreats, dominated by the personalities of saints and expressed in poetic forms. All of this Nora Chadwick summed up as the "Christian ideal in a sweetness which has never been surpassed."[17]

This golden age of the early Celtic church began in the fifth century and extended through the seventh or eighth century. A lesser, silver age would continue through the twelfth century before it fully gave way to a Romanized church, though still bearing some of its Celtic characteristics. Rural Ireland as well as Wales and Scotland took to these monastic communal centers as fitting their own tribal nature. The monasteries took the place of the ancient bardic and druidic foundations, and the monk was the new Christian Druid. Not all were drawn to these communal settlements for many would seek their solitude, at least for part of the time. Study, art, literature, poetry — all were part of this religious movement. Scripture, the singing of the psalms, a strong Trinitarian and Christological spirituality saturated their poems and prayers. The love of nature and animals pervaded all of it. Close spiritual ties, those of soul friends, united monks and monasteries.

Yes, I believe this early Celtic monasticism was dangerous. Full of passion and vitality, it must have challenged the local church and all of Christianity beyond it. Of course it had its dark side, too, of which we have hinted. Its severity will continue to emerge in later history and sometimes lead to fanaticism, intolerance, and self-righteousness. It is important to recognize that strain even while we maintain that this does not vitiate the brighter side of Celtic spirituality. Integrating the dark side of our lives rather than denying it is a challenge for us as individuals, as communities, and as a church. The past can teach us ways to enrich our lives in the present and also alert us to the pitfalls to avoid.

Chapter
Four

CRISES AND
CONTINUATION

HEN I VIEWED the old Celtic treasures at the Boston Museum, I realized that I had to find out more about the people who had given birth to such a culture. In the previous chapters I have set out some of my findings. Now I turn to my second question, which concerned the reasons for the disappearance of this culture and the emergence of a quite different culture and spirituality in the Irish church. Why did something so good and beautiful pass into history? I knew the English had taken control of Ireland and the Irish were still dealing with the consequences of that domination. But change had occurred much before the advent of the English. There had to be other reasons. And these reasons turn out to be quite diverse: theological problems, practices different from the rest of the church, and pressure points from within and without.

Celtic Doctrinal Controversies

Once the age of the martyrs had passed and the Christian church had gained acceptance, a succession of theological controversies consumed the church, bringing forth the first ecumenical councils. Most of the issues concerned the Trinity in general and the person of Christ in particular.[1] It does not seem that any of these great controversies were much of an issue in the developing Celtic church. The letter of Columban to the pope, quoted in the last chapter, does indicate that he, for one, was aware of such problems. The theological issues that caused concern in the Celtic churches, however, were not about the Trinity but about anthropology, the understanding of humanity.

Pelagianism and its derivative, semi-Pelagianism, remain code words for the heresy that imports in one degree or another the ability of the human being to achieve, or even contribute, to salvation without grace. In actuality, how much of that heresy goes back to Pelagius is uncertain. Pelagius, who lived roughly from 360 to 430, was a Briton and his birthplace was, like Patrick's, somewhere on the west coast of Britain. Pelagius was a Christian Celt who inherited the Celtic belief in faith and good works, in the holiness of all life, and in the power of the human, through asceticism, to achieve perfection. Pelagius went to Rome to study law, which he soon gave up in favor of devoting himself to the church. He found a great laxity of morals in the city and preached the need for an ascetic and spiritual life. In particular, he became a spiritual adviser to many, including a number of influential women.

Much of what we know of Pelagius comes from the writings of Saints Jerome and Augustine of Hippo, both of whom launched bitter diatribes against him. Few definitive editions of any of his own writings survive. But we surmise that he emerged in Rome as a theologian of note and as a man of great personal sanctity, moral fervor, and charismatic personality. He claimed that his ideas came from the Church Fathers; he himself adamantly opposed both Arianism and the Manicheanism that Augustine had formerly embraced. In combating the latter, Pelagius supposedly stressed the freedom of the human will as a right and responsibility. But what he actually taught, and what his disciple, Celestius, another Celt, taught in his name, is confusing and not easy to disentangle. In 411–12 the African church condemned Celestius as a heretic. The crux of the condemnation concerned the denial of original sin. Pelagius may or may not have professed this, but he did believe in *inpeccantia,* the possibility of living a life without sin through Christian effort, even though that would be a rare achievement.

The succession of events is hard to follow. Pelagius was conditionally condemned by Pope Innocent I and then pardoned by Pope Zosimus. Later the authority of the state was invoked, and Pelagius and Celestius were both condemned by an imperial edict in 418, in words reminiscent of the condemnations of Druids in former times. The decree with the exact terms of the condemnation was lost, and so there is much that remains doubtful. Pelagius was last seen in 420 in Egypt or Palestine.[2]

I believe Pelagius has something to say to us today if we can cut through the extremes to which the Augustinian criticisms may have pushed him. For an initial reassessment I quote M. F. Nicholson:

> Pelagius was the prototype of the Celtic missionary traveling the roads to distant cities, preaching Christian baptism, redemption.... Pelagianism was essentially a love of Providence, a denial of transmitted sin, an emphasis on the law of nature, on Christian ethics and asceticism, an enthusiastic striving for *inpeccantia* (sinlessness) and a peregrination for Christ.... The thought of Pelagius, as transmitted by the Irish missionaries and their heirs, helped to inspire optimism and the belief that human nature had, by God's grace, the capacity for improvement. These ideas were to play an important role in the early Carolingian Renaissance to follow.[3]

In their discussion of what God's grace was all about, the early Eastern theologians had stressed the freedom and graciousness of God. In contrast, Augustine changed the discussion into a stress on the sinfulness of humanity and our need for grace. It appears that Pelagius, and certainly his followers, was grounded in the Eastern tradition but got snared into playing according to Augustine's new game plan. Augustine hit home the basic inability of humanity to save itself, to do anything good without grace. In so doing he seemed to drive a wedge between the God of creation and the God of redemption. The Eastern and Celtic traditions believed creation to be a graced universe full of the grandeur of God. Augustine stressed the incapability of nature and creation by themselves to either know or find God. From a certain perspective, both positions seem correct, but extreme positions were taken and these overshadowed any possibility of agreement.

Augustine's theology led to a theory of predestination. From it also came a clearer enunciation of the doctrine of original sin as the natural condition of humanity. This doctrine eventually resulted in a belief that human nature was not only incapable of salvation without God's grace, but also incapable of doing anything good at all. A view of human nature as intrinsically debased evolved. Another aspect of this doctrine was the theory that original sin was passed on in the act of sexual intercourse. Such a belief, in turn, encouraged the recurring dualistic understandings of human nature that have plagued the church and led to a mistrust of matter, the body, and sexuality. The doctrine of original sin also led to the belief in "Limbo," perhaps never an officially declared doctrine but, nevertheless, a belief that had terrible practical consequences. Infants dying without baptism were believed to be forever deprived of God's presence. They were refused burial in the sanctified soil of a Christian cemetery.

The Celts must have had a terrible time accepting that. An indication of such a revulsion to the theory of Limbo can be found among the ruins of Glendalough. Here, on the outer rim of the monastic city, lies the remains of Saint Mary's Church (Teampall Mhuire), also known as the Nuns' Church and the Women's Church (Teampall na mBan). In a corner of the church grounds there is a plot of small stones marking the graves of unbaptized infants whom the women buried with dignity. While there I was told that in various places of Ireland today services of healing and the blessing of the graves in question are being held in an effort to erase this former belief and the harm it has caused.

The doctrine of original sin became dogma at the sixteenth-century Council of Trent. But many of the suppositions peculiar to that time no longer seem valid. Pope John Paul II has declared that the theory of evolution is entirely compatible with Christian thinking and that it is not necessary to see the story of Adam and Eve as a literal, scientific explanation of our beginnings. The belief that original sin is passed on by physical transmission, beginning with our first parents, is no longer tenable. In addition the new openness to other traditions and cultures and religions of the world, also promoted by the same pope, has brought to light differences with other visions of humanity.

In 1997 Father Tissa Balasuriya, a Sri Lankan priest, was excommunicated by the Vatican for his theological positions on Mary, grace, and original sin. It is possible that he had stepped too far outside of the Christian tradition. But it must be noted that he was trying to rearticulate the Christian tradition in dialogue with his Asiatic neighbors. The latter, like the Eastern church and the ancient Celtic church, do not accept the world and humanity as anything but basically and essentially good. The problems continue. Pelagius seems once again extraordinarily modern. I hope that the recent attempts to reconstruct his actual teaching can help us to grapple with these very contemporary issues. We may discover that even in the fifth century the real differences were not theological but cultural. We might enrich our understanding by learning from another culture without forsaking our own tradition and beliefs.

Back in the fifth century, however, the conflict of Augustine and Pelagius cast a shadow on the Celtic church and led to a recurring suspicion of heresy. Later Celtic theologians, proceeding from a different starting point, were also dismissed and denounced. The Celtic understanding was mystical, mythological, and symbolic. It would continue to clash with a Roman mindset that was often simpler, more straightforward, always practical, and sometimes literal.

Later, in the ninth century, John Scotus Eriugena would come from Ireland and achieve great theological preeminence in both Carolingian France and King Alfred's England. Eriugena was a philosopher and mystic who exemplified the Celtic insistence on a unified vision of all reality. He was perhaps the greatest speculative theologian in the West between Augustine of Hippo at the end of the patristic era and Anselm of Bec at the height of the Middle Ages. One of Eriugena's early works, *On Predestination*, denied the real existence of evil (for this would imply a dualistic universe) and denied that God would wish the death of any soul. He taught that neither sin nor punishment comes from God but from the sinner. This coincided with the teaching of Pelagius and his idea of a beneficent providence.

John was condemned at a local council (Synod of Valence, 855) and his writings dismissed as *Pultes Scottorum*, "Scots' Porridge."[4] However, his patronage protected him; he went on his merry way and continued his independent thinking.[5] His teachings had a profound influence on the symbolic mentality of the twelfth-century renaissance, and later on such mystics as Meister Eckhart, Tauler, Ruysbroeck, Nicholas of Cusa, Spinoza, and Hegel. I believe the Celtic tradition was once again offering its gift to the larger church of the day. Eriugena pointed the way to the reconciliation of creation and redemption, which have been separated in the West. Perhaps the Celtic tradition can render the same service today.

Conflict of Celtic Practices and Observances

If doctrine was the first tension point for the Celtic church, a second point was the area of practices, rituals, and observances. Here again I believe we are into a cultural clash more than a clash with faith or doctrine. Because Ireland never came under Roman sway it was able to preserve its own cultural identity and customs, and the Celtic pagan tradition was inculturated into the new Christian church. But when the two different Christian traditions met in the same country there was bound to be some conflict. A notable example of this conflict occurred at the abbey of Whitby in Northumbria, England.

From the time of Columcille's arrival in Scotland, the monastic foundation of Iona in the Hebrides had become a center of evangelization. The monks spread the message, in Celtic forms, south into northern England, notably Northumbria.[6] In the early part of the seventh century, King Oswyld (or Oswiu) of Northumbria took refuge at Iona. When he returned to his own country, he requested the community of Iona to send monks to establish a monastery in his own kingdom. So it came about that, in 635, the Irishman Saint Aidan, along with twelve monks, left Iona to settle on another island, that of Lindisfarne on the North Sea not too far south of the modern border that separates England from Scotland. There, for sixteen years, Aidan labored as abbot and bishop and was well known for his gentleness and care for the poor. Monks from Lindisfarne went to other areas of England, among whom were two English monks, Cedd in East Saxony and Chad at Lastingham on the Yorkshire moors. A friend and associate of Aidan was Hilda of East Anglia, who became the abbess of a dual monastery for men and women at Whitby.

With the arrival of the Angles and Saxons into England, the church of Rome recognized the need for further evangelization. Pope Gregory I decided to send a group of monks for this purpose and Augustine from Rome landed in Kent in 597, eventually to become the first archbishop of Canterbury. The Venerable Bede tells the story that the bishops of the Celtic churches welcomed Augustine and prepared to meet with him. They first discussed among themselves their position and practices, especially as these differed from the Roman tradition which Augustine would represent. They consulted a druidic hermit on how best to proceed. The hermit told the Christians that they should be open to working with Augustine and engage with him in dialogue. Then he supposedly told them that should Augustine stand and welcome them when they entered his presence, they would know that he would be open to them and accept them as equals. It happened that when they came to meet Augustine, he remained seated. They accused Augustine of pride. They were unable to come to any semblance of agreement, and the tension between the Celtic and Roman traditions in Britain was thenceforth destined to grow.

Now in the Celtic church there were certainly some significant differences inherited from its Irish monastic founders. Unlike the

urban centers of the continent, this was a tribal system with varying degrees of association or membership in the monastic family,
including lay members, married persons, and single people. Bishops
were part of the tribe as well, consecrated to be holy men rather
than authority figures, and there were often several in one monastery. But it was to be the ritual and liturgical differences that
would cause the confrontation between the two traditions.

One cause of tension was the manner in which the practice of
the tonsure was observed. The Celts had accepted a form prevalent among the Druids, who shaved the front part of their heads
from ear to ear, allowing the hair in the back to grow long. The
Roman tonsure was a shaved circle on the head surrounded by
some hair. But more significant was the controversy surrounding
the dating of Easter. Disputes on this issue were not constrained
to the Celts. There had been early differences in the methods of
determining the Paschal moon in the early church. The Council
of Nicea (325) determined one way to date Easter. But uniformity of practice did not prevail everywhere. The Roman date was
too early for the Celts, who believed Easter should be later in the
spring at the time of more light.

The Celtic celebration evolved from a grafting of Easter onto
the pagan spring feast of Beltaine, held around May 1 (in our cal-
endar system). Beltaine celebrated the sun god, Bel, and his gift
of fire to the earth. The druidic priest would light the Bel-tine, or
sacred fire, on the eve of this festival, all the others fires in Ireland
being extinguished. It was from this fire only that every other fire
would be lit for the rest of the year. Couples leapt over the fire to
ensure fertility and often married and mated at this time. At sun-
rise the Druid would lead the people to a hill to see the sun god
dance as he rose on the morn of that festival day.

It is believed that Patrick, in the story of his lighting the fire
on the hill of Slane on the vigil of Easter, was opposing the ritual
of the Beltaine fire on Tara and honoring the true sun God who
arose to dance on Easter morning. In fact his practice of lighting
the new fire would become part of the church's universal ritual of
the Easter Vigil, a practice which continues to this day. And Celtic
Christians, like their pagan ancestors, also climbed a hill on Easter

morn hoping to catch a glimpse of the sun dancing, some relating stories of seeing it do so.

It was this cultural background that made the celebration of Easter on a particular date so full of meaning to the Celts. It also helps to explain why any change would be opposed. Some have seen in Celtic resistance the old pagan culture refusing to change, and others have applauded it as a good example of inculturation. If we think this is an issue of the past and a matter of little importance, we have just to observe how the churches of the East and West continue to celebrate Easter according to different methods of dating. In 1997 the Roman and Reformed churches celebrated Easter on March 31; the Eastern Orthodox churches did so on April 27.

The controversy in the Celtic church might have continued indefinitely had not a particular development come about. King Oswyld of Northumbria had embraced the Celtic ways, which included the dating of Easter. His queen, Eanfred, was the granddaughter of the king of Kent and had spent time at Canterbury as a child. She came to Northumbria with a chaplain who followed the ritual and liturgical customs of Canterbury and Rome. The king and queen were celebrating Easter on two different dates! For the peace of his kingdom, Oswyld called a meeting to be held at the royal abbey of Whitby in 664 to hear the two sides and come to a solution.[7]

The outcome of this meeting is often summed up as a case of Rome suppressing the Celtic church. This is really a great oversimplification. Though this meeting has been known as the "Synod of Whitby" it really was not a Synod, as it was summoned neither by Rome nor by Canterbury. It was a *Witan*, a council called by the king, basically a political gathering of nobility and advisers at which the king would pass judgment by royal decree.

The spokesman for the Celts was Colman, bishop of Lindisfarne. He was supported by the abbess Hilda as well as by Cuthbert, who was then prior at Melrose and soon to become prior of Lindisfarne. The Roman cause was upheld by Wilfrid, abbot of Ripon. Wilfrid had once been a student at Lindisfarne but had not accepted the Celtic ways. He went off to Rome for further studies and returned "more Roman than the Romans," determined to stamp out the Celtic ways. He was a cleric in search of ways to impress the locals with the glory that was Rome. He also wanted to secure a suitable see in which to exercise authority himself. He did become the bishop of York, though not without difficulty and controversy. At Whitby Wilfrid argued the case before the king, portraying Colman as unloyal and disobedient to the pope, the successor of Peter. When Colman was challenged, he acknowledged the authority and primacy of the pope, and the king decided that the Roman customs would prevail in the kingdom of Northumbria. With the victory of Wilfrid, the Irish missionary movement in Northumbria and England effectively ended.

Colman returned to Ireland, bitter and defeated, though not before convincing the king to dispense Lindisfarne from the new Roman customs. Cuthbert, who was eventually to become bishop of Lindisfarne, was torn but loyal in working for the unity of the church. The Celtic church began to die out in southern and northeast England. It took a longer time for the newer practices to take hold up in the Highlands and over in Wales, where the Celtic Easter practices would continue, in some areas, up until the twelfth century. In Ireland the change occurred in a gradual, haphazard fashion, the south becoming more quickly observant of Roman ways than the north. But the change was inevitable, and the indigenous forms of Celtic Christianity gradually lost their preeminence.

Among the human casualties of this controversy I find the figure of Cuthbert most touching and inspiring. Known as "Cuddy" by the English of Northumbria, he was a Saxon who embraced the Celtic ways. He was a monk who wished to be a solitary but was constantly pulled into positions as prior, abbot, and bishop. Though saddened by the decision at Whitby, he strove for peace and reconciliation in the church. He finally resigned as bishop of Lindisfarne to spend his final years in a hermitage. Sought out both in life and death for his holiness, his body was eventually buried at the magnificent cathedral of Durham in 998, where his body became a center of popular devotion. I found his tomb behind the main altar to be an inspiring place to pray. Cuthbert touched in me, as in many spiritual seekers, the struggle for quiet and solitude even while trying to respond to the needs of God's people. He also speaks to me today as one who appreciated the beauty and wholeness of the Celtic Christian tradition and who would understand my desire to live it in our contemporary church.

Céli Dé and Monastic Reform

A third area of change in the Celtic church, more subtle than the first two, is to be found in its monastic life. The strength of its monasteries was central to the fervor, life, and spirit of the early Celtic Christian church. The golden age of Celtic monasticism (fifth–eighth centuries) exhibited both strength and weakness in its heroic, charismatic figures. These were strong men and women of passion, commitment, faith, and courage. The actual Rules directing these monastics and their communities were often sketchy, both in detail and program, because so much influence came from the personal power of the leaders. During the silver age of the Celtic church (eighth–twelfth centuries) the monasteries maintained their centrality. Dioceses and parishes did not take root before the twelfth century. The monasteries of this later time continued to produce people of great sanctity, scholarship, and culture. They could not always, however, live up to the high personal standards set by their pioneer ancestors. Abuses crept in regarding property and possessions, as well as in the use of power. Positions of leadership and influence were sometimes passed on to the sons and daughters of abbots and abbesses, or even to lay rulers and protectors, without regard to personal integrity or the ability to lead. The annals of the time also indicate that monasteries suffered from an increase of violence as the Celts continued their intertribal warfare; churches were burned, abbots and bishops murdered.

In eighth-century Ireland a reform movement was begun by monks called "Culdees," a name which is an anglicized form of the Irish *Céli Dé*, translated as friends of God or servants of God. The accredited leader of this movement was Maelruain from northern Tipperary, who founded the monastery of Tallaght, south of Dublin, in 774. There is an extant monastic Rule attributed to Maelruain. His reform demanded a return to a more severe asceticism and increased piety and learning. This movement was also characterized by a large increase in the anchoritic life as many monks chose to live some time, if not all their lives, in solitude as hermits.

This new resurgence of monasticism had much in common with its Celtic antecedents, but also bore the marks of the changes going on in the continental church. The emphasis on the daily praying of the psalter continued. The need for the *anamchara,* or soul friend, was also emphasized. A passionate commitment to the search for God and an intense religious longing expressed in prayer and discipline also characterized this period.

Other aspects of Celtic monasticism took on new significance. The Sunday observance was treated with new strictness with long liturgies, solitude, private prayer, and abstinence from work. Celibacy became a more central concern, sometimes in order to eliminate hereditary succession. We do not know when the practice of dual male-female monasteries died out. The evidence from the stone ruins at Glendalough indicates that a form of this was still alive in the ninth or tenth century. In this case it appears that a central core of a male monastic group was then surrounded by a ring of female monastics, still within the monastic city and more central than lay groups living there. There had also been some dual monasteries on the continent, and changes there affected the Celts. The patriarchal views of Roman society, the breakdown of order in the Dark Ages, the emergence of feudalism, the paternalistic well-intentioned desires of the hierarchy to protect women "for their own good" — all these led to a greater separation of men and women and a stricter cloister for women. The teachings of many church fathers, including Augustine, devolved into a certain suspicion of sex as well as other pleasures of the body. Even music became suspect in some parts of the continent, but this was more difficult for the imaginative and poetic Celts to accept.

Despite the loss of sensitivity to nature among many Christians on the continent, the sensitivity to the goodness of creation, the beauty of nature, and the immanent presence of God within all of created reality did prevail among the Celts. In fact, it received new attention in a wonderful and unique flowering of nature poetry combined with hermit poetry. A monk sings of a lark which accompanies his morning psalm. A wren is characterized as the bard which comes to join a monk's call for matins. The sea with its tides and playful seals is seen as God's handiwork. The cold of ice and snow of winter are described with a warning to birds to hide. The sun is greeted as the happy mother of the stars, rising like a young queen in flower. Still another monk wishes to be a stream gently rolling through a mountain pass. The imagery and sensitivity are quite beautiful.

Poetry was not the only written expression of the Celtic church at this time. Other literary pieces of this era include a number of monastic Rules, several Irish penitentials, numerous Lives of saints, and martyrologies. The Stowe Missal was composed in the early part of the ninth century (dated between 800 and 830), the oldest missal of the early Irish church to have survived. The missal contains extracts from the Gospel of Saint John, the rites of baptism, visitation of the sick, extreme unction, and viaticum, and a short treatise on the Mass, a commentary that is mystical and symbolic in nature. Also coming from this period are the great artistic masterpieces, such as the Book of Kells now on view at Trinity College in Dublin.

Monastic scriptoria continued their work. The annals of the time testify to Armagh, Glendalough, and Clonmacnois as being among the outstanding ones. Devotion to the real presence of Christ in the sacrament is a mark of the age. Pilgrimages to monastic sites within the country became more common. Toward the end of the eleventh century pilgrims were attracted to Station Island on Lough Derg in County Donegal. According to legend this was the site where Saint Patrick had a vision of Purgatory. Severe penitential exercises were associated with these pilgrimages and, at times, they were excessive. These included fasting for the weekend, deprivation of sleep, and going barefoot while processing through the night, even in cold and rain. In 1497 Pope Alexander VI ordered the cessation of pilgrimages and the destruction of "Saint Patrick's Cave." A modern commentator on the Irish spiritual scene, John O'Riordain, has wittily observed that

> if the truth were told, far from ordering its destruction, the same Alexander Borgia might well have derived a considerable and much needed spiritual uplift from a trip to the renowned penitential station.[8]

Weekend pilgrimages to this site continue to this day, and they are attended by many young people, showing the tenacity of this ascetic impulse in the modern Celtic Christian. Nowadays, it is also possible to undertake a shorter one-day pilgrimage there.

The passionate and ascetic expressions of the Celtic monastic church were not lost during the silver age of the Christian church. If anything, they tended to become more rigorous and even extreme. Penitential practices such as fasting, vigils, standing in cold water, keeping the arms extended in a cruciform fashion (the "cross-vigil"), emulating Christ on the cross, became more common. Although there was also an increased skepticism toward pilgrimage away from the home country, the practice hardly died out. A short poem from the ninth century conveys this theme:

> To go to Rome,
> great the effort, little the gain,
> you will not find there the King you seek
> unless you bring Him with you.[9]

The prayers of this period are gentle and tender, and there is little separation of the religious and the secular. There is often a playfulness as evidenced in another ninth-century poem of a scribe speaking to his cat, named Pangur Ban, comparing his own work in searching for words with that of the cat searching for mice. In this playful banter lies the scribe's own insight into the practice of *Lectio Divina,* the monastic method of prayerful reading of the scriptures. We thankfully have this poem preserved because the scribe, perhaps in his own prayerful distractions, wrote his thoughts down in the margin of a commentary on Greek and Latin writings.[10]

The eighth or ninth century is the probable date of what has become known as "Saint Patrick's Breastplate," or "the Cry of the Deer." Although it is written in a later form of Irish and therefore could not have been written by Saint Patrick himself, this prayer encapsulates what is best in Patrick and Celtic spirituality. It is a prayer enmeshed in the Trinity, in the immanence of a loving God, in the goodness of a created world alive with the power of God. The image of the breastplate reflects the theme of protection so important to a people who lived close to nature, very aware of its dark and destructive moods. These breastplates, or *Lorica*, were becoming an increasingly common genre of prayer at this time. This is a prayer of closeness and tenderness. Many people are familiar with only the one stanza about the closeness of Christ ("Christ beside me, Christ before me, Christ behind me, Christ within me, Christ beneath me, Christ above me . . . ") but the entire prayer deserves close examination and reflection. I offer here two stanzas to capture the spirit of this prayer. These verses express, first of all, a unique view of the closeness of God in creation, a view not to be found so clearly expressed outside the Celtic world until the Canticle of Saint Francis of Assisi in the thirteenth century. The extract also expresses another important theme of Celtic spirituality, the immanent and close presence of God in the ordinary happenings of everyday life.

> For my shield this day I call:
> Heaven's might, Sun's brightness,
> Moon's whiteness, Fire's glory,
> Lightning's swiftness, Wind's wildness,
> Ocean's depth, Earth's solidity, Rock's immobility.
>
> This day I call to me:
> God's strength to direct me, God's power to sustain me,
> God's wisdom to guide me, God's vision to light me,
> God's ear to my hearing, God's word to my speaking,
> God's hand to uphold me, God's pathway before me,
> God's shield to protect me, God's legions to save me:
> from snares of the demons, from evil enticements,

> from failings of nature, from one man or many,
> that seek to destroy me, anear or far.

This is a traditional nineteenth-century translation reworked by Noel Dermot O'Donoghue, a wonderful modern Celtic visionary, an Irish priest who became the first Catholic to teach theology at the University of Edinburgh. Here is his commentary on the Breastplate:

> We are here at a central insight of Celtic theology. . . . Christ comes not to show up or illuminate the deformity of a fallen world but rather to release a beautiful and holy world from bondage; most of all to release the human person, body and soul, from bondage, and to dissipate the shadows that lie across all creation through the presence of the enemy and his dark angels. The new light of Christ is an enabling light allowing the original glory of creation to glow and radiate, not a new light to take the place of that original light. . . . So it is that the asceticism, sometimes extreme, that goes with this tradition, is not the expression of a human righteousness confronting the righteousness of Christ, but rather an affirmation, difficult but possible, of an original righteousness which is the created image of the eternal Father and the all-holy Trinity.[11]

The *Célí Dé* monastic movement embodied both the development and the continuity of this time. The monks of this movement attempted to live the full Christian life with a new idealism, freshness, and vigor, even if at times they were excessively austere and even puritanical. Their continued influence on the Celtic character cannot be underestimated. It is unfortunate that the movement was not able to continue to affect, at an institutional level, the ongoing renewal of monastic and church life. I believe there were two reasons for this. On the continent, and also in Britain, the Rule of Saint Benedict was everywhere replacing the ancient Celtic monastic Rules and practices. This happened partly for political reasons. The Rule of Benedict was utilized in the Carolingian empire to bring order and stability in the face of great centrifugal forces that tended to divide the church. But Benedict's Rule also had internal advantages of moderation, a realistic sense of humanity, and the practical, nitty-gritty approach to community living that did not depend as much on charismatic leaders to keep it going. The disadvantage to this, it may be conjectured, was a certain loss of imagination and flair that the more poetic Celts brought to the monastic movement. I tend to believe that some interplay of the two monastic movements would have been fruitful for the church in the same way as the interplay of Roman and Celtic Christianity can enrich each other. The fact was that the Rule of Benedict was often imposed on Celtic monasteries.

However, there was also another circumstance, entirely external to the church and monasteries, that brought about a reversal to the momentum of the reform movements. After the fall of the Roman empire, the Celtic countries had been left alone to develop in their own unique way and preserve their own culture. Now the first of a succession of forces from without would disturb that insularity. I refer to the arrival of the Vikings.

The Viking Invasions

The center of the *Célí Dé* movement, the monastery of Tallaght, founded by Maelruain in 774, had become the center of a union of reformed monasteries, known as the Oentu Maelruain. In the year 795 the first of a succession of Viking raids from the north came to an island off the shore of Dublin. It was not long before these Norsemen were plundering monasteries. Tallaght, though not immediately destroyed by this new invasion, was severely weakened. Just when the reform movement was bringing about a renaissance of art, literature, learning, and spirituality, it was cut off in the bud and never was able to reestablish itself in its original vigor.

A number of internal reasons, mostly economic, brought about the great expeditions of Norsemen from the Scandinavian lands. They set off in their long ships headed for all the coasts and rivers of Europe. Down the western coast of Europe they came, launching attacks on the Orkneys, Shetlands, Hebrides, Isle of

Man, Scotland, Ireland, and Wales. Prior to 830 these attacks were only sporadic. After this time the attackers came with a more determined effort to set up Scandinavian colonies. In Ireland they founded the first real urban centers in the seaside towns of Dublin, Arklow, Waterford, Wexford, and Cork, and in the river town of Limerick. They attacked and plundered many of the Irish monasteries, absconding with treasures and magnificent works of art, now on display in Scandinavian museums. It is true that the Irish had themselves plundered monasteries in the Celtic tradition of intertribal warfare. The coming of the Norsemen precipitated the first real efforts of the Irish clans to unite against a foreign enemy instead of engaging in the usual cattle raids on each other.[12]

The Viking invaders circumnavigated the entire island and attacked Skellig Michael off the Kerry coast as well as the monastery on the Isle of Inishmurray off the Donegal coast. During the years 830 to 860 and 910 to 930, the Irish suffered terribly at the hands of the invaders. After 930 the Irish began to turn the enemy back. The battle of Clontarf in 1014, led by the imperial Brian Boru, signaled the end of the Viking invasions.[13] The Vikings turned elsewhere, sacking, for example, the center of Saint David's in Wales in 1088 and Iona in Scotland on numerous occasions during the ninth through the eleventh centuries.

In Ireland, the Norse people were being accepted and assimilated into the Irish social landscape. This was one of many assimilations over the centuries in which the Celtic character prevailed, even while making adjustments. The Vikings brought with them to Ireland an enrichment of Irish commerce with their shipbuilding and trade; they introduced coinage in 997. For a while the native Irish left them to their new cities, themselves preferring to remain rooted in a rural society with its own particular social, legal, and religious structures. As the newcomers from the north gradually became Christians, intermarriage began to take place, and the Norsemen lost their identity as a separate people.

Though the copying of manuscripts continued in Celtic monasteries, the raids seem to have brought an end to the production of illuminated artistic masterpieces and a diminution of monastic metalwork. Some Irish left their native land to pursue cultural and academic possibilities on the European continent. Among them were Sedulius Scotus and John Scotus Eriugena.

Different materials were used to rebuild the destroyed monasteries and other structures. Most of the ruins and monuments extant today come from this period or later. The simpler wooden buildings and the fortified island crannog settlements of preinvasion times have not survived. The change to a greater use of stone ensured that many of the new structures would survive. Such, for instance, are the *raths,* or ring forts; some of these may have predated the Vikings but most of those extant date from post-Viking times.

Celtic High Crosses and Towers

This new age of the Vikings brought notable changes to the church architecture of the time, producing many of the structures whose remains pilgrims visit today. To minimize the threat of fire, churches and shrines for saintly relics were built of stone instead of wood. A major innovation in church structures was the erection of the great stone crosses, or "high crosses."

> High crosses may be considered as Ireland's greatest contribution to the monumental art of medieval Europe. They are not confined to Ireland and get their alternative name "Celtic crosses" from the fact that they are also frequently found in parts of Britain...Scotland and Wales...and in the north of Britain as well. Ireland, however, has the finest and most varied selection of such crosses anywhere in these islands.[14]

Some high crosses may predate the coming of the Vikings. But their number increased after this time, and some, no doubt, were built to replace many older bronze crosses which had been looted and removed. Others were erected as boundary markers, as indicators of sacred places, as recorders of some historical happening or agreement, as tools to teach biblical stories, and also as places of prayer. These are truly "high" crosses, some of them as high as twenty feet tall. They are sculptured with scenes, mostly from the

High Cross at Monasterboice, Co. Meath.

Bible, but also from the lives of Saints Paul and Anthony, favorite heroes of the desert. One study of these crosses has found a remarkable concordance with the biblical scenes found in frescoes in the continental churches dating from the time of Charlemagne, thus suggesting that these outdoor crosses were substitutes for frescoes not found in the simpler Irish wooden churches.[15] The inspiration for the selection of scenes depicted for both might well go back to the churches of Rome.

Most of these crosses are from the tenth century. The best examples are the cross of Muiredach and the west cross, both at Monasterboice, the market cross and the broken cross at Kells, the cross of Durrow, and the cross of the scriptures at Clonmacnois. At Iona, where the Vikings had devastated the ancient monastery, the wonderful Celtic crosses of Saint Martin and Saint John can still be seen today.

A distinctive feature of these early crosses is the circle or ring around the junction of the horizontal and vertical bars of the cross. This may be simply structural and pragmatic, a way to reinforce this point of intersection. Even if this be so, the Celtic imagination would see more. The circle may represent the sun, a vestige of old Celtic worship, but also a sign of the cosmic Christ, or it may represent a garland of victory for the figure of the victorious Christ. Perhaps it is even the symbol of the union of creation spirituality and redemption spirituality. Two hundred years later, in the twelfth century, there appeared another series of high crosses. The ring on these crosses is not as prevalent as in the earlier group. The type of cross that typified the post-Norman church is less dramatic and unique. However, the ringed Celtic cross eventually experienced another revival in the nineteenth century, largely for nationalistic and political reasons, as an expression of the resurgence of a Celtic identity.

The second major form of church structure to emerge during this time was the round tower. This structure is archetypal of Ireland, found almost exclusively there except for three other known examples, two in Scotland and one on the Isle of Man. Some stand as high as 120 feet, their tall, tapering shape often topped by a conical cap. Their entrance doorways are usually about ten feet

High Tower at site of St. Bridget's Monastery, Kildare (present site of St. Bridget's Anglican cathedral).

above the ground. It has often been assumed that these structures were built for protection against marauding Vikings. Though they may have been used for this purpose, it is now generally agreed that the original intention was religious in character. Bells were probably rung from the top windows of these towers, known in the Irish language as *cloicthech,* meaning a bell house or tower. They were similar to the Italian campanile or to the Islamic minaret, whose purpose was to call the faithful to prayer. They were visible for some distance and often served to mark the presence of a monastery to approaching pilgrims. A celestial symbolism might be part of the design as well, and there was some nineteenth-century conjecture that these round towers were Phoenician fire towers, stylite columns, or even phallic symbols. Today about sixty-five such towers remain in Ireland, in varying degrees of survival.[16]

In my study of the years following the heroic age of the beginnings of Celtic Christianity I discovered that while some characteristics and practices did change, many of the original features of Celtic Christianity endured. The decline of charismatic leaders, the periodic wane of monastic fervor, the influences from the Roman and continental church, the increase of lay power and influence — all of these contributed to various changes. But the basic vision perdured: creation is graced by God and by the immanence of this God; creation is filled with God's presence and with the presence of those who have died and are now in the bosom of God. The Celtic propensity for intense religious longing endured. A mythic and imaginative stance toward the world continued to be expressed in the great outpouring of literature and art.

The Vikings came and stayed. Towns, buildings, and commerce were improved. All of this certainly affected the Celtic church and particularly the monasteries. No matter how things were changing around them, however, there were still many people living an intense Christian and holy life. The Celtic church had withstood the doctrinal controversies such as Pelagianism and persevered in its own distinctive, imaginative, creation-based spirituality. It had adapted some of its observances to the Roman tradition, especially after the Synod of Whitby, and yet its distinctive monastic church organization still prevailed.

So my question about why this Celtic Christian church eventually disappeared was still not fully answered. I was learning that the more difficult challenges still lay ahead.

 **Chapter
Five**

Decline

ELTIC CHRISTIANITY as a distinct institution of the larger Christian church lasted until the early twelfth century. Celtic Christianity as a worldview and spirituality endured within the larger church in the ensuing centuries. I believe that there was a progression of events which particularly changed the Irish worldview and led to new expressions of spirituality. The three principal factors that I perceive to be responsible for the more contemporary expressions of spirituality in Ireland are the Cromwellian colonization of Ireland in the seventeenth century, the penal laws of the eighteenth century, and the great famine of the nineteenth century. I want to show how important they were in leading to a new church and a new spirituality. To do that, however, brings us quickly from the eleventh to the seventeenth century and I find it necessary to first consider the more gradual changes that took place in those intervening six centuries.

The Irish, a clannish and conservative people, could not but be affected by the coming of the Norsemen and the Danes. This opening to people of a different culture also led to the greater influence of external forces from the continent. Europe as a whole had become a feudal society with power centered in many local lords. The church emerged as the strongest and only real universal authority under powerful and centralizing popes. Monasticism also became more centralized under the influence of the Benedictine Abbey of Cluny, which spread its reforming arm outward. This was supported by Pope Leo IX (1048–54), who brought the monasteries more directly under the control of the papacy. This led to a system of periodic check-ups through canonical visitations. Pope Gregory VII (1073–85) implemented various reforms concerning simony, celibacy, divorce, lay investiture, and other matters that would challenge Celtic practices. The next pope, Urban II (1088–99), himself a monk of Cluny, pushed the Gregorian reforms even further.

The new urban centers of Ireland established by the Vikings began to look to the continent for the example of urban society and government. It only stood to reason that the church too would have to be part of this structure. The Norse king Sitric I of Dublin in 1038 built Christ Church in Dublin, a church destined to be a cathedral in need of a bishop. To avoid the control of the Celtic monks, the bishop-designate was sent to be consecrated by the archbishop of Canterbury.[1] Waterford and Limerick did the same. This precipitated the influence of this English see on Irish affairs, which would result in the active interference of the archbishops Lanfranc (1070–89) and Saint Anselm (1093–1109). The Irish church was now open to the influence of English and continental churches. Thus began the reform of the church in Ireland and the movement to conform to the continental forms of church organization.

Church Reform in Ireland

With a growing awareness of the model of continental churches added to the pressure coming from the archbishop of Canterbury, the church in Ireland convened a local synod in 1101 at Cashel and another in 1110 at Rath Bresail. The result of these meetings was a new church structure. After seven hundred years of a monastic church, the country was now divided into two archbishoprics, Cashel and Armagh, each with eleven suffragan dioceses under them. For the first time in history, the Christian church in Ireland was organized on the same pattern as the continent, in dioceses and parishes. A later synod, at Kells in 1152, carried out more reforms and also bestowed primacy on the see of Armagh. The bishop now had authority over parish and monastery. Cashel was subject to Armagh. All were subject to the bishop of Rome.

It took forty years or more for these changes to have any real effect. Old monastic centers continued to have their influence. Some of them, like Clonmacnois, themselves became episcopal sees. Archbishop Cellach of Armagh became an early reforming agent, but it was the man he chose as his successor, Malachy (1094–1148), who had the more lasting influence. On the way to Rome to seek the pallium for the archbishops of Armagh and Cashel, he met Saint Bernard of Clairvaux in France and came under the latter's influence. Bernard had little respect for the Irish people or church and, when writing a biography of Malachy, he wrote:

> Malachy understood that he had been sent not to men, but to beasts.... Never had he found men so shameless in their morals, so wild in their rites, so impious in their faith, so barbarous in their laws, so stubborn in discipline, so unclean in their life. They were Christians in name, but in fact they were pagans.[2]

John O'Riordain believes Bernard was given to some hyperbole in his assessment of the Irish and notes dryly,

> While admitting guilt on many counts, Ireland cannot have been as bad as St. Bernard claims, since it produced St. Malachy himself, whose person, spirit and general disposition so patently captivated the saint of "Clairvaux." Bernard, brought up in the tradition of Roman law, was quick to see any other legal system as barbarous, but the Celtic church in Ireland had shown enough independence of

spirit to adopt Christianity without exchanging the Brehon Law [the ancient Irish legal code] for the Roman code.[3]

Malachy wished to stay with Bernard and become a Cistercian monk but was persuaded to return to Ireland to implement reform. Of special significance was his introduction of both the Cistercian and Augustinian orders to Ireland.[4] This was the move that would break the power of the old Celtic monasteries. In 1142 some Irishmen trained as novices at Clairvaux under Bernard were sent, along with other French monks and stonemasons, to begin the building of a new-style Cistercian monastery at Mellifont. Of this move, the De Paors write:

> It was finished in 1157 and an assembly of kings and bishops attended the consecration of the completed abbey church. It was of a type previously unknown in Ireland, a building two hundred feet long, not set in the midst of a cluster of cells, but part of the Cistercian complex of communal buildings: dormitories, refectory, chapter house, cloister, cellars. . . . It was the foundation of Mellifont that marked the end of the Irish monastic era.[5]

Malachy returned to Rome a second time but was never to return to Ireland. Stopping at Clairvaux on his return trip, he died in the arms of Bernard on November 2, 1148. The saint of Clairvaux honored Malachy by writing his life, and decreed that at his own death (which would occur five years later) he would be buried next to Malachy in front of the high altar at Clairvaux. I see Malachy as a rather sad figure, a person who did not appreciate his own Celtic identity sufficiently to preserve and develop it. I also wonder whether he doesn't represent a recurring phenomenon seen then and today — a tendency for a small, peripheral, or different culture to forsake its own "soul" in order to be accepted in a larger, more powerful society. Many small countries in Africa, Asia, and even Europe seem to be too easily adapting Western and specifically American mass culture forms, to the neglect of their own rich history and tradition.

There are, however, other figures who seemed to appreciate

and honor their own rich tradition. Such a person in the same twelfth century was Saint Lawrence O'Toole (1128–82), abbot of Glendalough (1153), where he introduced the Augustinians. Lawrence represents a time of transition. He became the first Irish archbishop of Dublin (1162), his predecessors all being Norsemen subject to the archbishop of Canterbury. Through his enlightened leadership, Dublin became a real part of Ireland, no longer just a Viking settlement; here, the Celtic propensity to prevail and incorporate newcomers was apparent. His influence on the pope on behalf of the Irish church and his championing of local causes displeased King Henry II, whose invasion of Ireland (in 1169) came while Lawrence was archbishop. When Lawrence was in England, King Henry refused to allow him to return to Ireland. Lawrence died in Normandy and was canonized in 1225. There would not be another Irish-born bishop of Dublin for many years.

The old Celtic tradition lived on in the erection of more high crosses. Increasingly, the ornamentation favored scenes of the crucifixion or, in some cases, figures of bishops. Examples of these structures still stand at Kilfenora, Roscrea, and Glendalough. Irish stonecarvers also turned to the ornamentation of the new stone churches. Cormac's Chapel at Cashel, consecrated in 1134, was one of the first of these stone buildings. An early imitation of Cashel was the church at Kilmalkedar, County Kerry. The remains of this church, with its interesting outdoor cross, Ogham stone, and carved sundial, continue to attract visitors and are well worth seeing. A distinctively "Irish Romanesque" style emerged in architecture at the "Nuns' Church" at Clonmacnois, Clonfert Cathedral, and the cathedral of Tuam. The figure of the human head, an old motif of Celtic art, shows the tendency to return to older patterns and can be seen dramatically depicted on the arch of the doorway at Dysert O'Dea and on the carved doorway at Clonfert.

The old monasteries had been the preservers of learning and even in the twelfth century produced great manuscripts. These include the *Book of the Dun Cow* and the *Book of Leinster*. From these we have the earliest records of ancient Celtic lore, including the great epic known as *Tain Bo Cualnge* — the Cattle Raid

*Sundial and Ogham Stone at Kilmalkedar, sixth/seventh century mo-
nastic remains near Mt. Brandon, Dingle Peninsula, Co. Kerry.*

of Cooley. These older monasteries also produced beautiful metal-work, including Saint Patrick's Bell, the crosier of the abbots of Clonmacnois, Saint Lachtin's arm from Kilkenny, and the Cross of Cong, which enshrined the first recorded relic of the True Cross in Ireland. All these artifacts are now preserved in the treasury of the National Museum in Dublin. Other reliquary shrines are found in the British Museum and elsewhere. A number of poems, prayers, litanies, sermons, and homilies testifying to the faith and spirituality of the age are also extant. Bardic schools of poetry are mentioned as early as 1041 and more and more frequently in the annals of the following centuries. In an account written in 1580 it is said that bards fasted and prayed before writing religious poetry. This was the beginning of the age of the troubadours, the age of the Arthurian myths and the various accounts of the Grail legend. Change occurred, monasteries became continental in style, but there was still much that exemplified the old Celtic tradition.

The Anglo-Norman Invasion

In addition to internal church reform, the twelfth century witnessed a major cultural upheaval in Ireland with the coming of the Normans from England. Historically this was, of course, a momentous happening as it brought the English to Ireland for the beginning of an eight-hundred-year stay, an event which continues to unwind to this day. Sadly, the Normans came because of one of those recurring Celtic fault-lines playing itself out, namely, the Irish fighting among themselves. Diarmuid MacMurchada, king of Leinster, had been driven from his kingdom in one of those incessant interprovincial wars. He fled to Britain in 1167, where he made a bargain with some knights in south Wales who agreed to help him regain his kingdom in exchange for grants of land in Ireland. The first knights arrived in Bannow Bay in County Wexford, defeated the Irish, and awaited reinforcements. The principal invasion came in 1169; the Normans took Wexford, Waterford, and Dublin, and soon were in the midlands. Henry II came to Ireland in 1171 to assert his authority and to support the Norman knights.

Despite the pleadings of Archbishop Lawrence O'Toole, Henry convinced the English pope, Adrian IV, to grant him rights over Ireland for the sake of church reform. In 1175 the king concluded the Treaty of Windsor with the Irish "high king" Rory O'Conor, who pledged to pay an annual tribute while Henry agreed to leave O'Conor as high king of any territory not conquered by the Normans. But Henry did not honor this agreement and continued to confiscate more and more land.

The Normans fortified the towns, brought social organization and order to them, and built great castles, towers, and moats to secure their lands. The Irish for centuries had been decentralized politically, choosing the close, intimate texture of family and clan loyalties. Marked by a tenacious and conservative character, they had, nevertheless. developed an advanced form of civilization in their literature, art, thought, law, and custom, and a form of the Christian church that reflected a people never part of the Roman empire. Now the Norman presence was slowly but surely to lead to a new reality. The De Paors sum up this transition:

> The Normans, in spite of their initial success, never conquered Ireland. There was no tradition of allegiance to a central authority and the country could only be conquered *tuath* by *tuath,* but the invaders too soon became involved in the complexities of Irish alliances to accomplish this. In the centuries that followed, many of them became totally absorbed into Irish society, abiding by Irish law and speaking the Irish language; only a thirty mile deep bridgehead around Dublin remained as a secure base for English law and custom in Ireland. But with the invasion of the high-kingship, Irish monasticism, and Ireland's political and cultural isolation came to an end.[6]

This period certainly had its effects on the Christian church and people's spirituality. First, there was an architectural development as Gothic cathedrals began to appear, representing a move away from the simple people-centered and nature-centered mentality. Christ Church in Dublin, founded in the eleventh century, was rebuilt as a Gothic cathedral around 1235, and nearby Saint

Patrick's Cathedral was completed in 1254. In 1250 Saint Bridget's Cathedral was built on the site of her former double monastery in Kildare, and in Kilkenny Saint Canice's Cathedral was completed in 1260. Other Gothic churches were built in Galway, Youghal, and Limerick.

With the coming of the Normans, the native Irish lost control of the sources of power. Much of the church history of the twelfth through the fifteenth centuries concerns a series of squabbles over the sees of archbishops and bishops. Though explicitly forbidden by the pope, the English policy became one of excluding the Irish from ecclesiastical dignities. As each see became vacant, the English set up their own man as the successor. Peter Harbison comments on this period:

> Indeed, the distinction between the "church of the English" and the "church of the Irish" was the fundamental social and political reality of later medieval Ireland. In certain instances where a diocese had a reasonable balance of Irish and English inhabitants, special deans or deacons would be appointed where the two different languages were spoken. One Archbishop of Cashel, a learned savant, Michael Scot, resigned after only two days because he could not understand the language of most of his flock. By the end of the thirteenth century a greater number of sees were occupied by Englishmen, particularly after Connacht had come into Norman hands in 1235.[7]

Though in some ways the saying about the Normans that "they became more Irish than the Irish" is true, many still remained English in their heart and allegiance. Many absentee bishops spent more time in England than in Ireland. In some places the reforms that had begun so effectively were now being undermined. The same reality, unfortunately, also occurred within religious orders. The Cistercians, begun so strongly, divided into monasteries with Irish and English abbots. In 1227 Stephen of Lexington in the "Conspiracy of Mellifont" removed all abbots of Irish origin and made English and French the languages of Cistercian Ireland. Here was another area in which the Irish were losing control of their own house and their ability to hand on their own spiritual insights.

New forms of life were also brought to Ireland with other continental orders. In 1224 the Dominicans founded a house in Dublin and quickly spread to other towns, though there would not be an independent Irish province of the order until 1484. Their ministry was principally that of preaching. The Carmelites, introduced into England by the Crusaders from the Holy Land, were established by 1271. A third group were the Augustinian Friars who arrived at Ballintubber Abbey in County Mayo in 1216.[8] The new friars were associated with the "School of the West," a kind of traveling workshop of masons and sculptors. Their work is associated with foundations at the Cistercian houses of Corcomroe and Boyle as well as the Augustinian houses of Ballintubber and Cong. These churches and monasteries are some of the more highly ornamented buildings west of the Shannon.

But it was especially the Franciscans, coming to Ireland about 1226 at Youghal, who would have the most influence on the future of the Irish church. They preferred to be in the cities at first, gradually moving out into rural areas. They were singularly noted for their closeness to the people. In later centuries they would be much appreciated for their solidarity with the people in their darkest hour of persecution and oppression. Few names are known of those early friars. Perhaps their anonymity testifies to their success in staying poor and simple and not set apart from the people. We do know, though, that some were scholars, for a number of friars became bishops.

The Franciscans, however, also exemplified a characteristic of the age already mentioned: the tension that continued between the English and Irish churches. As the friars moved into rural areas, they attracted Irish-speaking native vocations. This had mixed results. Louis McRedmond observes:

A cross-fertilization took place: the revitalizing of religion on the continental model in rural areas, the infiltration of preaching by Irish symbolism — the redemption won by Jesus becoming an *eiric* or blood-price, the Christian pursuit of holiness being equated with the hard discipline of young men on the military maneuvers of the Fianna. Sometimes there was a happy junction of sentiment, as in the love of nature, of birds, of trees, which was as distinctively Celtic as it was Franciscan.[9]

But racial tensions entered friaries too. McRedmond quotes a certain Brother Simon who is supposed to have said that it is no more a sin to kill an Irishman than to kill a dog. Even religious houses, particularly those of Normans, were targets for raids and looting by the native Irish. But to their credit, many Franciscans respected the spirituality and native gifts of the Irish, learned their language, and used the prayers of the Celtic tradition. They also welcomed lay people into their Third Order of Saint Francis, which became very popular with the Irish.

And so the Christian church continued, the living faith of people existing amid changing structures. One tradition of Celtic piety, pilgrimage, endured as a spiritual phenomenon. The Cistercian Abbey of Holy Cross in Tipperary, originally built in the twelfth century, was rebuilt by 1405 and found new life as a center of pilgrimage. Ballintubber Abbey, situated on the path of pilgrimage of Saint Patrick's route to the holy mountain of Croagh Patrick, also became a pilgrimage center as did places like Glendalough and Clonfert.

The medieval devotion to Mary that blossomed on the continent also found its way to Ireland. In the thirteenth century alone we know that fifty-one churches and monasteries were built and dedicated to Mary. The cross and the passion of Jesus became large in the consciousness of Irish piety with a propensity to seek reparation for sin and the mercy of God. I notice here an influence on Irish spirituality from a continental spirituality which had a more pessimistic view of human nature and was preoccupied with original sin, quite different from the old Celtic vision. This pessimistic view grew in part out of the fourteenth-century Black Death and the ensuing tendency to see life on earth as difficult to bear. In this view, there was little happiness to expect in this "valley of tears." On the other hand, on a more positive note, sacred scriptures retained an important place in the writings of the time in Ireland, and the psalter remained the basic book of prayer. Coupled with a love of scripture was a living sense of the mystical body of Christ. The fourteenth-century *Leabhar Breac* (Speckled Book) states that commentators spoke of the "body of Christ" in three meanings — the human person born of the Virgin; the church as the assembly of believers united to their head, Jesus Christ; and the holy scriptures which set forth the mystery of Christ.

Penance and fasting, hospitality and the love of nature were other positive aspects of the people's spirituality that endured, along with some unhealthy elements including superstition and numerous abuses of celibacy and marriage. The twelfth century had been that of reform. By the sixteenth century there was need again for such reform not only in Ireland but throughout the church. The great schism and era of antipopes (1378–1417) weakened the papacy and the church and brought much confusion. Crusades and Inquisitions might have seemed helpful at the time but they resulted in more problems than solutions. Poverty, ignorance, and the poor training of the clergy were widespread throughout the church. Witch hunts, suspicion of mystics like Meister Eckhart, the trial of Joan of Arc, and the selling of indulgences were among the causes of a religious cataclysm that would touch all of Europe and the Celtic countries as well.

The Protestant Reformation

The Reformation had different effects in the diverse Celtic countries. Martin Luther's revolt against Rome and John Calvin's break from Rome in 1533 had little meaning for the Irish, a little more for the Welsh, but much for the church in Scotland. After Margaret of Scotland began the reform of the church there according to Roman lines, her son David I (king from 1124 to 1153) established the diocesan system over the monastic one and brought in new religious orders from the continent, similarly to how it was happening in Ireland. The course of the Scottish and Welsh churches from the twelfth through the sixteenth centuries roughly paralleled what we have seen in Ireland, except that the Welsh and Scots had a closer, more entangled, relationship with England.

John Knox, former chaplain to Edward VI in England, fled from the regime of Mary Tudor to Geneva and came under the influence of John Calvin. Knox returned to his native Scotland in 1559 and the next year, as rector of Saint Giles' Cathedral in Edinburgh, founded the Reformed Church of Scotland along Presbyterian lines, abolishing the authority of the pope and forbidding the celebration of Mass. The Celtic church was practically dead. The puritanical aspect of the new religion was quite antithetical to much of the old wild and free spirit. In writing of this change, Anthony Duncan, an Anglican canon of Scottish descent, laments:

> The focus of religion was effectively shifted from the heart to the head. In Scotland, popular education became a religious crusade, for the people must be enabled to read their Bibles and think for themselves. Not only was the intellectual climate essentially non-mystical, it speedily became positively anti-mystical. The intuition was suspect — it became regarded as the realm of the devil and his angels. In Scotland alone, over the course of two and a half centuries, between four and five thousand people were to be burned alive for a "witchcraft" which was often as not little more than the possession and use of higher than usual degree of intuitive perception.[10]

The Reformation in Wales took a different trajectory. In 1066 the Norman invasion of England also touched Wales and reopened the Church of Wales to English and continental influences. As in Ireland and Scotland, the twelfth century was the time of the establishment of dioceses and parishes, the overshadowing of the old Celtic monasticism, and the introduction of new Roman religious orders. In 1639 the "Nonconformity" movement began at a "gathered church" at Llanfaches. It embraced popular education and was dependent on itinerant preachers. But it was Welsh Calvinistic Methodism, as preached by Howell Harris (1714–73), that would take root. At first, as its founders John and Charles Wesley had intended, this was considered to be part of the Church of England. Eventually, however, in 1811 its followers broke away. The English-speaking in Wales tended to be Tories and Anglican, their bishops all Englishmen. The Welsh-speaking were either Nonconformist or Methodist and included many radical tenant farmers, miners, and industrial workers. The Welsh language was officially forbidden in public and legal usage in 1536, but it continued to be used, along with old Celtic practices, in the more remote mountainous areas of the country. Unlike Presbyterianism, Methodism with its evangelical revivalism seemed to have some coordinates with the Celtic vision as well.

But in Ireland the picture was quite different from these two closer neighbors to England. Though England had taken possession of Ireland in the Norman invasion of 1169, there was little influence for some time other than the participation of the newly arrived Normans in local happenings. By the time of King Henry IV (1399–1413), England was already too busy with other concerns in Wales and elsewhere to interfere much in Ireland. The Anglo-Normans in Ireland prospered and maintained their allegiance to the king. In 1494, however, a law was passed in England limiting the Irish Parliament's authority to pass laws as well as curtailing the right to assemble and meet. This enactment, known as Poyning's Law, would limit the independence of the Irish Parliament for the next three hundred years. Opposition to England waxed and waned. In 1534, the same year that Henry VIII set himself up as head of the new Church of England, open opposition to England was voiced at a meeting at Saint Mary's Abbey in Dublin. This resulted in Henry's determination to subjugate the Irish and oblige them to adopt his new church. Forty Irish and Anglo-Irish lords submitted to him with lip service, but there was little change in the practice of their Catholicism. In 1536, the English-born archbishop of Dublin, George Browne, pressed through the Irish Parliament the Act of Supremacy, recognizing Henry as head of the Church of Ireland, which was now the official church. There was little enthusiasm among the people for this move. Henry had himself declared "king of Ireland" in 1541.

Between the time of Henry VIII and Elizabeth I, definite moves were made by the Catholic Church to implement the reforms of the Council of Trent. Jesuits came to Ireland in 1642 for the first time and joined the friars in the counter-Reformation movement. In many ways the content of the Protestant Reformation never really became known to the Irish. Even when Catholics accepted Henry's supremacy, they had little interest in his doctrine. The annals continue to report regular sacramental anointings and penance at death. Only in towns, particularly within the Pale (the English enclave centered in Dublin), was there any acceptance of Reformation doctrines. It is in the poetry, the imagination, the music of these Celtic Irish that we discern what was really felt. During the reign of Elizabeth I an Irish bard named Costelloe sang of his hope for Ireland in a sad poem called "Roisin Dubh" (Dark Rosaleen). This is a poignant call to keep hope and believe in justice before the judgment hour. "Oh, my Rosaleen, my dark Rosaleen," the poet repeatedly calls on her, "do not die, do not die."

Meanwhile, educational possibilities within Ireland were very limited, especially after the collapse of the old monasteries. But between 1578, the year of the foundation of the Irish College in Paris, and the end of the seventeenth century more than thirty Irish colleges were set up throughout western Europe. The use of the printing press allowed the spread of spiritual books in the native Irish tongue with poetry often being used to summarize doctrine and to help memorize it. In 1647 the Vincentian Fathers came to Ireland and settled in Cashel and Limerick. Proceeding along the lines that they had used in rural France, they began to preach missions, which were well accepted by the people.

The dissolution of the monasteries took place between 1534 and 1539, but this too was implemented slowly in Ireland, principally at first only within the Pale. Little of Henry's Reformation affected Ireland for the next twenty years. Pressure abated under Edward VI, who succeeded Henry. By 1555 even England had been reconciled to the papacy. Ironically, it was a Catholic sovereign, Mary Tudor, who began the move to subjugate the Irish in order to incorporate them more thoroughly into England and its traditions. The Irish language and customs were deemed to be obstacles and in need of replacement. The move to suppress the

Irish identity, its traditions, and its particular spirituality had now begun in earnest.

The real change would occur with the reign of Queen Elizabeth I (1558–1603), who was determined to crush Ireland and the Catholic Church. She brought "planters" from England and created new settlements in the south and the midlands. The natives of Munster staged a revolt with the help of the Spanish but were defeated at Smerwick (Dingle Peninsula) in 1579–80. Another revolt and Spanish invasion were defeated by the English at Kinsale on the coast of Cork in 1601. Under Elizabeth, almost all Catholic church buildings were taken over, except for some in rural areas. Her successor, James I (1603–25), brought more planters from England and Scotland, his own countrymen who he claimed "could skip around the bogs as well as any Irishmen." They settled mainly in Ulster, thus sowing the seeds for major problems that would occur later. The old Brehon laws, which grew out of Celtic society and had governed Ireland since the seventh century, were abolished in 1606. The O'Neills and O'Donnells, aristocratic families of Ulster, sailed to exile in Spain in 1607 and left many of the common people without native leadership ("The Flight of the Earls").

External force lessened again under King Charles I, who followed James in 1625. There was much support from the Irish for this new "king of Britain and Ireland" who wished to realign the English church more closely with traditional Catholicism. But Charles was overthrown in 1642 and beheaded in 1649. Civil war had broken out in England when a Commonwealth was declared by Parliamentary "Roundheads," a group of radical Puritans. The leader of the movement was Oliver Cromwell (1559–1658).

All this may sound complicated, but it is part of the story that led to the three major events that I alluded to at the beginning of this chapter, namely the Cromwellian colonization, the time of the penal laws, and the famine. In looking at the Protestant Reformation and its effects in the Celtic church, I am most struck by Ireland's unique position. All over Europe, peoples tended to adopt the religion of the ruler. In countries such as Italy, Spain, and France, where the rulers remained Catholic, the majority of the people remained Catholic. In northern Germany and the Scandinavian countries, as well as in England, Scotland, and Wales, where the ruler became Protestant, most of the people became Protestants. But in Ireland the people would not give in to the new religion. Perhaps a lot of grief would have been spared had they done so. The determination to preserve their old Catholic faith led to major suffering in the ensuing centuries.

**Chapter
Six**

The Darkest Hour

E COME NOW to the final pieces in this development of the contemporary Celtic church. In this chapter I trace the most negative developments in the story of the Celtic Christian church and its new distinctive spirituality. These are developments that are often sad and distressful. They are sometimes glossed over in historical and ecclesiastical reviews. Such neglect has come, at times, from the pain associated with the happenings and the wish to excise them from memory. Moreover, to avoid guilt or responsibility, there has at times been an unwillingness to acknowledge the reality of some of these events. I believe it is very important to look at these developments of the seventeenth, eighteenth, and nineteenth centuries in order to see their ramifications for our times. We have lived with these realities but often, out of ignorance, have turned to either blame or dismissal of what we perceive to be the facts. In this book I have looked at a rich spiritual tradition hitherto unknown to myself and many others as well. A much narrower Christian tradition took root, and today many dismiss it as negative, guilt- and shame-

based, or at least an inadequate spirituality for our times. It is too easy, and avoids the full issue, just to blame England, Rome, priests, or parents. This is not the full story. Some positive aspects of these times will also be reviewed, but I ask you, as you read this chapter, to understand that we are isolating the negative perspectives in order to come to a fuller understanding of the story and to open up our own options for the future.

I look, first of all, at the Cromwellian colonization, passing then to the time of the penal laws that followed the victory of King William at the Battle of the Boyne. Then I survey the famine, "The Great Hunger" of 1845–50, not with the intention of getting a complete picture of its political, economic, and nationalistic causes and results, but mainly to see how it affected the psyche, mores, and spirituality of a people. Finally I look at the new church that emerged and the type of spirituality expressed in it. The latter included particular developments for women and men and changing attitudes toward sexuality. All of this is background for understanding the religion and spirituality taken by the Irish immigrants to their new countries in the Diaspora.

The Cromwellian Colonization

Charles I was king of Great Britain and Ireland from 1625 to 1649. Civil war broke out in England in 1642, eventually leading to the execution of Charles. Oliver Cromwell (1599–1658), a member of Parliament since 1640, shared the religious and political views of the Puritan Party, which he combined with the fervent spirituality of the "Independents" (Congregationalists). Seeing the civil war as a religious struggle, Cromwell led the army and revolt against Charles and was eventually declared the "Lord Protector," a king in all but name.

Cromwell marched into Scotland and subdued the people there. Then he turned to Ireland. The Irish had engaged in periodic uprisings, sometimes attacking the new colonists who had come since Elizabethan times. In 1642 some Irish insurgents had even established briefly the "Irish Catholic Confederacy" with a parliament at Kilkenny. Cromwell was determined to put a stop to all such movements and to demand an account for killings of English citizens, the new colonists, and recompense for the damage inflicted on their property and belongings.

To a country already beset by local wars, periodic famines, and pestilence there now came a time of slaughter and repression. In the years of Cromwell's colonization, 1649–60, some 504,000 Irish people perished by sword, plague, famine, and economic hardships.[1] Cromwell began with the siege of Drogheda in 1649, when 3500 people were killed. He then slaughtered 1500 in Wexford, including women and children. Then it was on to Limerick and Galway. He attacked priests and forbade the Mass and went on a large-scale pogrom of destruction and murder in a series of massacres. The author of the seventeenth-century *Cambrensis Eversus* noted the following:

> Under the Protectorate it was death to harbour or protect a priest; death not to disclose their hiding-places "in the caverns of the mountains, the chasms of the quarry, and in the dark recesses of the forest." And "any person accidentally meeting and recognizing a priest was subject to have his ears cut off, and to be flogged naked through the town, if he did not inform." "Many a time," says Bruodin, "were these iniquitous laws enforced in Ireland."[2]

When the choice was made to refrain from killings, other punishments were found. Prison colonies of priests were set up on Inishmor and other islands. Undesirable men as well as poor women and children would be put on ships and sent as indentured servants to the American colonies of New England and Virginia. Others were sent into slavery in Barbados. It is estimated that as many as 50,000 Irish were thus banished from their land. Finally it was decided to transplant all nonconforming Irish to the west side of the Shannon River, to the province of Connaught and County Clare, where the poorest soil in Ireland was found. Many actually were transplanted, though it was impossible to carry out the plan fully. Lands were confiscated and given to those who backed the war financially and who subscribed to the Protestant Reformation.

In 1530 the native Irish and Norman-Irish owned 100 percent of the land. This would drop to 59 percent in 1641, 14 percent in 1703, and 5 percent by 1778. In seeking out those who fled and hid, forests were denuded, never to recover.

I believe all of this had profound spiritual results. This was a people of the land, a people who believed their connection to the earth to be holy and sacred. Now they were uprooted. Now they were strangers in their own land. Their clans were broken up, effectively ending the practice of common ownership of their property. A people who shared all, to whom hospitality and common life were natural, now struggled to survive. A sense of dignity, of self-worth, of freedom — all were attacked. Deep cleavages on religious grounds resulted as mistrust and fear led to resentment and hatred. Peter Harbison comments:

> The slaughter and destruction which Cromwell and his generals brought about in Ireland in a few short years, between 1649 and 1652, has left an indelible and long-lasting memory in the Irish psyche, and makes it difficult for some Irish to understand how the English honour Cromwell by having his statue outside the Mother of Parliaments at Westminster.[3]

Cromwell had little effect in eradicating Catholicism. In fact he may have been instrumental in bringing about what had never happened in Ireland before, a uniting of the people in opposition to an external force. And this brought a particular unity of identity to Irish Catholics and their practice of the faith.

The Eighteenth-Century Penal Laws

Ireland enjoyed a temporary peace after the death of Cromwell during the new reign of Charles II (1660–85). In fact, during this time, Dublin began to make its mark for the first time in English literature. It was also the time of the reerection of earlier high crosses, such as at Dysert O'Dea and the market cross of Kells. Then Charles was succeeded by James I in 1685, who was defeated by William of Orange at the Battle of the Boyne in Ireland (1690–91). James fled to France, where he died in 1701. The result of this in Ireland was the Treaty of Limerick, which acknowledged certain rights of worship and property for Catholics. When the treaty was not honored, a rebellion broke out but was crushed. The defeated Irish "Wild Geese" went to France in exile.

Two centuries of oppression and intermittent resistance ensued. Poverty deepened as a considerably increased population depended on areas of poor agricultural sustenance. Many lost both land and human dignity. Even when and where the practice of the old religion was permitted, it was lived by a people who had been degraded and humiliated. Open opposition was sporadic. In 1678 Titus Oates claimed to have uncovered a "popish plot" to bring in a French army of occupation. This led to the arrest of Luke Wadding, the bishop of Wexford, who was eventually released because of good Protestant connections. However, Peter Talbot, archbishop of Dublin, died while in prison and Oliver Plunkett, archbishop of Armagh, with a number of others, was executed at Tyburn in England in 1681. Repression increased after the Battle of the Boyne. In 1697 the Dublin Parliament passed a measure entitled "An Act for Suppressing all Fryeries, Monasterys, Nunneryes, etc." It was called, for brevity's sake, the Banishment Act and decreed that all religious order clergy as well as all Catholic bishops should leave Ireland by May 1, 1698. This marks the beginning of the penal days.

Until 1717 various penal laws were passed against Catholics in England and even more so in Ireland by the Irish Protestants under English control. The laws were of irregular severity and enforced to varying degrees at different times and in different places, as even many Irish Protestants found them abhorrent. One diocesan priest was allowed to remain in every parish as long as he swore allegiance to the English sovereign, with the expectation that the priest would not be replaced after death. Order priests often stayed in defiance of the law or registered as diocesan priests or pretended to be laity. Franciscans as well as others continued to be visibly present, often using farmhouses in which to found their friaries.

To exclude Catholics from any public office, an oath rejecting transubstantiation (the Catholic doctrine of the change of bread and wine into the body and blood of Christ) was demanded of all candidates. Similar oaths were required by many professional and municipal groups. The ancient practice of *gavelkind* was now inflicted on the Irish by the English. This demanded that a person's estate be equally divided among all male heirs, thus reducing the size of properties. Nor were Irish permitted to buy land. Fines and levies were leveled against Catholics for any kind of damage resulting from war or civil disturbances. Much that was done was justified by pointing to the French and Spanish who did similar things to Protestants in their countries. A notable difference was that in Ireland the majority of the people were oppressed in their own country.

Mass was forbidden at various times and places, and secret nocturnal gatherings in forests at "Mass Rocks" were inaugurated. A bounty was placed on the heads of priests, and "priest hunters" sought their capture. In Kerry in 1753 the following scale of rewards was registered: thirty pounds sterling for a priest; fifty for a bishop; forty for a vicar general; fifty for a Jesuit. There are stories of priest hunters calling for a priest under the guise of wanting the last sacraments and then turning him in. A great story is told at the present-day Ballintubber Abbey in Mayo. Near the church is a large cemetery with many graves. In the midst of this graveyard is a large dead oak tree. The story tells of a Sean 'A Sagart, a priest hunter in the eighteenth century. For every priest's head he got five pounds, which he then spent on drink. Finally in 1726 he himself was killed, and his body was thrown into a lake. The priest ordered him to be buried in the graveyard. However, the people would not give him a Christian burial, that is, facing the east and the rising sun. They gave him a pagan burial, facing the north. The oak tree is supposed to have grown right out of his grave, but the tree was, in time, hit by lightning!

The result of all the restrictions, particularly those on priests and religious practice, was to increase the people's devotion and fidelity to the Mass. Attendance at Mass increased dramatically from this time, and great reverence for priests also became part of the people's religious attitude. Priests were as poor as the poorest people and often served at the threat of their lives. Little Mass houses were to be found everywhere, simple little hovels which the people built to assert their right to worship. Nor did the proverbial Celtic wit desert them. An oft-quoted poem from the period compares the foundation stone of the Catholic Church with that of the Protestant Anglican Church, portraying the latter as coming from the loins of Henry VIII.

John O'Riordain wryly comments that with such sentiments imbedded in the race-memory, it may take much longer for ecumenical dialogue to occur in Ireland than elsewhere. But also to be recalled is the fact that some Protestants, for example, Jonathan Swift, dean of Saint Patrick's Cathedral in Dublin (1713–45), spoke out on behalf of Catholics.

By 1778 the first Catholic Relief Act was passed, allowing Catholics to take longer leases and giving them some stability as tenants. Irish hopes were raised when pressures on England to lighten up on the Irish came from the American War of Independence. Revolution in France also brought aggravation to a head. England received criticism, as well, from European Catholic countries for their treatment of Ireland. The first native seminaries were allowed to open in Ireland, first in Carlow in 1793 and then in Maynooth, the National Seminary, in 1795. The English strategy was to allow small favors to stem the demand for greater ones. For the English there was always a perceived danger of a backdoor invasion of England by Spain or others through Ireland.

The final outcome of all these stresses was the suppression of the Irish Parliament by William Pitt. He effectively dissolved Ireland as a separate country in the Act of Union, which took effect on January 1, 1801. Periodic talk and promises of a "Catholic Emancipation" from all the penal laws brought Catholic acceptance of this move, which they thought might better their lot. The bribery of many members of the Irish Parliament to vote for this measure also lay behind the acquiescence of the Irish. Now there was no Ireland and would not be until 1922. Immigrants, such as my grandparents, coming to new lands in the succeeding century would be noted as subject to the "Queen of Great Britain and Ireland." The situation would not really change until Daniel

O'Connell came on the scene and Catholic Emancipation became a reality in 1829. Some things would begin to change for the better, gradually, but only in some areas. And in the midst of all these problems a huge catastrophe was about to descend.

The Great Hunger (1845–50)

The Cromwellian persecution and the consequent penal laws brought great suffering to the people, dislodged many from their homes, drove them into deeper poverty, and severely undermined their sense of self-worth and well-being. It is true that a few Irish were well off, particularly those who exercised a trade in urban areas. But Ireland in 1841 was still largely a rural society: only 20 percent of the people lived in towns and only 5 percent in cities with a population over fifty thousand. The west of Ireland, in particular, had been newly developed into a heavily settled farm area. This must be seen against the background of a population which grew from 3 million to 8.5 million between 1700 and 1845. These figures alone betray a culture of poverty because frequently the less people have of material goods, the more they treasure their human resources and the consolation of their children, who may eventually have to support them. Present-day welfare opponents in America complain about the poor having more babies but can't seem to understand what a culture of poverty is all about.

Ireland had seen times of blight and famine before the 1840s. But the larger population now living on this small island, many of whom for various reasons depended on the potato for basic sustenance, would make this famine far worse than previous ones. People lived close together in rural areas in a *clachan* and *rundale* system. A *clachan* was a group of farmhouses where all landholding was organized communally. People might have their own vegetable gardens by their houses, but they also shared the space of a few strips of growing area in a large enclosed field. This system was called by the Scottish name *rundale*. Thus, although these people were very poor materially, they lived in a community of strong mutual support, a community with a rich oral culture of singing, oratory, dancing, and storytelling. Hospitality to outsiders was also part of this system.[4] The famine would attack not only their stomachs but their entire tribal and communal way of life as well.

The blight, caused by potato fungus, spread with devastating speed, destroying one-third of Ireland's crop in 1845, three-quarters in 1846 and 1847, and one-third in 1848. At least one million people died and two million emigrated within the next two decades. Much of the discussion of this phenomenon seeks to blame the English government, a blame perhaps to be shared, to a lesser degree, with some Irish landowners. Certainly the episode contributed greatly to growing Irish nationalism and opposition, even hatred, toward England. Only recently has much thought been centered on the damage done to the Irish themselves, both those who survived in Ireland as well as those who emigrated, to say nothing of those who died directly from this blight. This was a monumental disaster and brought such pain, such suffering, that many could not possibly deal with it directly but continued nonetheless to live out its effects. Only with the sesquicentennial commemorations of 1995–2000 would there appear the beginning of open, objective, and scholarly treatment of the famine. The centennial anniversary in 1945 occurred at the end of the Second World War, which had its own devastating effects, and it was not the time to face the horror of the famine. Similarities are sometimes drawn with the experience of the Afro-American community in the United States both in the effects of the original event (in this case, slavery) on succeeding generations and also in the inability to deal with the original event for about 150 years afterward.

The most extreme British opinion interpreted the famine as a direct divine punishment on Ireland for its sin of popery and for the laziness of its people. It was a blessing in disguise, some English claimed, by which the old Irish ways could be eradicated and a real civilization could come to Ireland. The Act of Union in 1801 had made Ireland part of Great Britain, but poverty had actually grown worse. There had to be some way to explain this, so the Irish themselves must be to blame. And some Irish accepted this judgment and saw the famine as a divine punishment. Indeed the famine did eradicate the old farming ways and brought Ireland into a more modern agricultural future — but at what a price! Along with the famine came the clearances, or massive evictions, in which people were turned out of their hovels, moved to poor houses, or simply left homeless, their homes burned and destroyed.

Almost a half million people were evicted during the famine years. The reliance on each other broke down as there was nothing to share. Guilt for failing in the old ways of hospitality and for turning away not only neighbors but also other family members intensified their sense of degradation. They felt that they had failed in some fundamental human way. Guilt, shame, a profound sadness, a sense of failure as parents and providers were effected in those who survived. There was a harshness in family relations that developed as well, a new bitterness dividing people who were used to sharing all. The fuller results of the famine are summarized by Seamus Deane, Keough Professor of Irish Studies at the University of Notre Dame:

> ...the death of almost a million people; mass emigration; a steadily declining population; Malthusian "moral restraint" in marriage patterns (necessary in a culture where contraception was disallowed or almost unheard of); the marginalization of the Irish language; the disappearance of the culture of the Irish peasantry; the steep rise in the influence of the Catholic Church.[5]

Those who emigrated were also affected by the famine. A wake was held for them as they departed, for they were not expected to be seen again. They left the tribal, rural life to begin life anew, but quite differently, in the urban areas of England, Scotland, Australia, and North America. The pain became a distant memory soon to be replaced by romantic and unreal memories of a culture that was no more, or even of a country and ways that never existed. Denial of pain gave way to happy stories of the old country, the old sod and sentimental songs with images that few people back in Ireland could ever recognize. These circumstances, both in

Ireland and in the Irish Diaspora, profoundly affected the religious life of the church and the people's spirituality after the famine.

The New Irish Church

Following the Reformation, most countries adopted the religion of their rulers. The Latin maxim was *cujus regio, ejus religio* (whose region, so his religion). That was not the case in Ireland. The Anglican Church became the official "Church of Ireland," and it remained so until disestablished in 1869, even though at the time it represented only one-eleventh of the population. The Catholic Church, however, emerged from the penal times and famine even stronger than before with its adherents clinging to it with great fervor.

Things were a bit simpler, but not entirely easier, in other Celtic countries. It took some time for the Presbyterian Church to prevail as the "Church of Scotland," with a separate Anglican Church also in existence. But by 1690 there were Scottish penal laws discriminating against both Catholics and Anglicans. The intolerance toward Anglicans dissolved, and Catholic Emancipation there took place in 1793 with the Catholic Relief Bill. Catholics became a very small minority, living mostly in the Highlands. The collapse of the Irish rebellion in 1798 brought many Irish Catholics to the areas around Glasgow in the lowlands, and there was another sharp increase in their number from those fleeing the Irish famine. The result to this day is that the Catholic population in Scotland, certainly in the lowlands, is largely of Irish ancestry. Another blot in the history books is the time of the Scottish Clearances in the early nineteenth century. Many poor farmers in the Highlands were removed, even violently, from their homes to allow for their lands to be used for the raising of sheep.

In the eighteenth century, at the time that the Welsh Methodist Church was becoming the dominant religion, many Irish emigrated to Wales. Catholics were emancipated there in 1829, coinciding with the emancipation in Ireland. The "Church of Wales," Anglican, was not disestablished until 1920. The eighteenth century saw some cultural advances in the Celtic tradition in Wales. In 1751 the Cymmrodorion Society was founded to encourage Welsh literature, science, and art. Poetry abounded, and in 1789 an Eisteddfod, a competition of poetry and music, was held, leading three years later to an annual festival and thus reintroducing what has become today's bardic tradition.

In Ireland both the Anglican and Catholic churches claimed continuity with the ancient Celtic Christian church, but both needed external influences to maintain their position and develop. The Anglicans had their backing from the Church of England with which they were one after the Act of Union of 1801. The Catholic Church depended more and more on the influence of Rome and the post-Reformation churches of the continent. As a result, much that became known as "Irish Catholic" was, in fact, quite alien to the Celtic church of previous centuries. O'Riordain comments:

> It is unfortunate that of all the fifteen hundred years of Christianity in Ireland, its "public image," so to speak, should have been taken from the nineteenth century, which in many ways was probably the least "Irish" and indeed, the least "Catholic."[6]

To be sure, not all of the old disappeared even if the new church did oppose. Thus pilgrimages, pattern days (feast days of patron saints), holy wells, and wakes were part of a rural spirituality that went back to pre-Christian days and were often joined to partying and drinking. These practices were part of a monastic and agricultural culture in which veneration of local saints and their shrines was very important. Now the need to find respectability within modern society (dominated by the "Protestant Ascendancy") and also a respectability vis-à-vis the Catholic Church as it had developed on the continent after the Reformation caused some embarrassment over the old ways. The external influence intensified because many young Irish men had gone to European centers, in particular to France, to be ordained as priests at a time when this was not possible in Ireland.

It was the priest who would be the key to the reforms in the new Irish church. This was a natural development because of the high esteem in which the clergy were held by the laity. They had stayed close to the people, suffering with them in persecution, in penal times, and during the famine. Some had given their lives, and many served in constant risk of death or imprisonment. The courage of the clergy became a symbol of the defiance of the people in holding on to their old faith. A Frenchman in Ireland in 1839 observed that the Catholic clergy were the only persons in Ireland who loved the lower classes and treated them with esteem and affection. The number of priests increased, particularly in the second half of the nineteenth century. This led to a great outpouring of missionary priests going to all areas of the globe — Africa, Asia, South and North America, including many American dioceses in need of priests.

As the church became more institutionalized after the famine, a new pattern developed: the priest began to consider himself a man set apart. He was to make an annual retreat and appear to be different by dressing in black with a Roman collar. As a result, clericalism and a more authoritarian priesthood slowly emerged. While the great majority of priests were good pastoral men, there were some domineering ones also. At a mission in Dingle in 1846, the priest used a whip to keep the queue for confession in order![7] Priests began to exercise great influence on both the social and political life of the people. One Maynooth professor taught that a priest in dealing with an uneducated congregation should give instruction from the pulpit on how to vote, and claimed that it was a moral obligation of an uneducated man to vote as his priest directed him. No doubt the priest was often the only educated person, sometimes even the only literate person, in the local communities. Unfortunately, this implied only a minimum of learning and understanding. A certain anti-intellectualism became a feature of this new church. Maynooth National Seminary was for a good part of its history a place where intellectual excellence was hardly prized.[8] Seminarians had little access to newspapers and periodicals, enjoyed inadequate library facilities (there was no artificial light in the main library until the 1960s), and their training emphasized silence, penance, and withdrawal from the world.

The principal function of the priest was to dispense the sacraments. He was believed to be the main means of salvation. His duty was to "read the Mass,"[9] hear confessions, and anoint the dying. And priests generally did this very faithfully with a profound belief in the ritual. However, in line with much of post-Reformation spirituality, the Mass was often seen as something the priest did for the people who, in turn, were passive, quiet, and private in their response. Because of the secretive nature in which the Mass had to be celebrated in times of persecution, this quiet and passive way of attending Mass was perhaps particularly evident in Ireland. Attendance at Mass was a sign not only of one's orthodoxy but also of one's Irishness. A religiosity based on obligation grew strong. A frequently found pattern was to pray at Mass, but not to pray the Mass itself. Many pious souls prayed the Rosary during Mass, and Rosary beads wrapped around the hands during Mass became a sign of such piety. Even after death this pious practice was repeated by placing the beads in the hands of a believer in the coffin.

Sacramental celebrations of the church were most consonant with the sacramental view of the world that was part of the Celtic mentality, but now many forms of post-Reformation piety were brought to Ireland from the continent, some of which were quite new and foreign to the Celtic spirit. Priests educated in Rome and other continental centers liked to bring back practices they had learned, such as devotion to the Sacred Heart, May devotions, forty hours devotion, the Novena of Grace, the Three Hours Agony, First Fridays, and numerous novenas. Along with these came scapulars, prayer books, medals, holy pictures, prayers that never failed to be answered, and Rosary beads. Most of the new prayers were in English since the use of the Irish language had diminished, partially because the Irish themselves wanted to fit into the society of the English-speaking. As John O'Riordain comments, there is nothing wrong with any of these and all can be of spiritual help, but "its greatest weakness, to my mind, is that it did not appreciate nor take account of the people and their tradition." And then O'Riordain quotes from a Tomas Uasal de Bhal:

So it comes down that to our time our piety has been of the eighteenth century, Georgian in style and pattern rather than Gothic or Gaelic; our formal praying has been, so to speak, a kind of period-piece, more suited to the squares and broad streets of Dublin than to the Irish countryside....One is loath to be critical of so venerable a corpus of prayer and piety but may one most respectfully suggest that it may be too sustained where it should be a little more spontaneous, too civilized and urban where it should be a bit bedraggled and daring and rural, too elaborate where it should be inspired, too flat and level when it should be soaring to the skies, too articulate and too fully stated for the Celtic mentality, for which, as Kuno Meyer said, the "half-said thing is dearest."[10]

This European piety contains little that is poetic, imaginative, or musical but tends toward literalism and a vision of reality as simply black or white with no gray areas. There is little awareness of the oneness with the natural world and of God's grace of creation. There is little acknowledgment of the scriptures, which were considered too Protestant to be embraced (and at times were used by Protestants to try to convert Catholics). Devotion to the Sacred Heart is an example of what I mean. No doubt the picture of the Sacred Heart has become almost synonymous with an Irish home. And there is much in it to respect and appreciate. For many this image has become a symbol of God's unconditional and limitless love for us. Devotion to the Sacred Heart is known to go back to the time of Saint Gertrude in fourteenth-century Germany. It became a popular French devotion with Saint Margaret Mary Alacoque in the seventeenth century. The Irish took to this devotion as part of the new post-famine spirituality. The essence of this devotion was not new and could be seen in the biblical image of the Good Shepherd. But the change of imagery is significant. The image of the shepherd in the gospels, a development of an Old Testament theme, is that of a God wildly in love with his people, searching for the lost, the wounded, even the runaway. This theme comes out in other images in the gospel, such as the father of the prodigal son, a parent who loves his child unconditionally no matter what he or she has done. Nor will this parent allow the child to be humiliated to come back into the family embrace.

These were the images that had stimulated the early Celtic monks. They were God-intoxicated people, passionately searching for the face of their God in a love affair, emptying themselves in severe ascetic practices, not to punish themselves, but to be purified in order to allow God to live within them. Nor did they cease to relish their humanity, their love of learning and of life, even when they had little of material goods. Contrast this to the image of God that many in the Christian world developed after the medieval plagues and the Irish, even more so, after the famine: we must have been bad and God has forsaken us; we must do something to earn God's love back.

This later spirituality centers on a God who requires satisfaction and reparation. Perhaps it is an unfolding of the theory of atonement by satisfaction that Saint Anselm introduced in the eleventh century. In this theory, God demanded the death of his son as the only possible adequate satisfaction; now we must do reparation for our sins as satisfaction in order to regain God's love. For many, the Sacred Heart was the symbol of this hurt God in need of reparation. This was my experience growing up in Sacred Heart Parish in New York. Following the visions of Saint Margaret Mary, the stress was on "making nine first Fridays,"[11] and on doing penance and reparation. And the artistic representations add to this feeling. A new type of religious art developed which was literal, symbolic only in its identifiable sameness of portrayal and colors (red for the Sacred Heart, blue for Mary, brown for Joseph). A whole plaster art industry followed. How different from the Eastern respect for the icon, which is a labor of the artist's love! And how different from the ancient Celtic love of line, symbol, and abstraction. This in itself shows the dualism at work here. Religious art now must represent the "other" to be holy, that is, it must be something other than human, other than beautiful and artistic by human standards.

The sacred and secular have been separated; a sacramental view of reality is no longer at work and the Incarnation is more an abstract doctrine to be believed than lived. God is not immanently present in the ordinary, in the everyday, in the very human. God is out there somewhere. And this is a God who demands reparation. A whole piety around the "poor souls" in purgatory emerged, concerned that these loved ones could spend next to forever in pain and suffering unless we make reparation for them. This is a new piety, and some may say it is a perfectly legitimate development. It may well be a beautiful spirituality for some. But it must be recognized as quite new and alien to the Celtic mentality.

The nineteenth and early twentieth centuries were a time for building up the institutional church in Ireland in conformity with Roman and post-Reformation practices. As many as two thousand churches were built or rebuilt in this period. A system of parish schools was introduced. Institutions of education and charity proliferated, and many new religious groups were introduced. Religious orders provided the possibility of education for many. In 1775 Nano Nagle founded the first native institute, the Presentation Sisters of Cork, to educate the lower and emigrant classes. The Irish Christian Brothers, founded by Edmund Rice in 1802, had 43 schools with 7500 pupils in 1838 and by 1862 ran 181 schools attended by 20,280 students. In 1816 the Irish Sisters of Charity were founded to teach in schools, to nurse the sick, and to house the poor. The Irish Sisters of Mercy were founded by Catherine McAuley in 1827 and, under diocesan control, flourished in their work of education, visitation, and nursing of the sick and ministry to those in work-houses, to female prisoners, and to women in difficulty. By 1881 they had 170 convents. Confraternities, such as those of the Christian Doctrine and of the Blessed Virgin, enlisted lay people to educate the poor in the faith. Many lay people joined the Third Order of Saint Francis. The Catholic Truth Society was one of many groups disseminating Catholic literature (in the English language) all over Ireland. The Legion of Mary was founded by Frank Duff, who, with Edel Quinn, enrolled many lay people in a movement of piety and apostolic mission. This was truly a time of fervent and breathtaking activity in the church.

With all these developments the church was becoming more unified and centralized. The directives of the Council of Trent were being implemented. In 1850 the Synod of Thules set standards for parishes and schools in 189 decrees. Paul Cullen, archbishop of Dublin from 1852 to 1878, helped to stamp this pattern of centralization on the church in conformity with canon law. He initiated the custom of the nuptial Mass, a move away from the practice of having sacraments in the home, which had been the Celtic norm. Pilgrimages, visits to holy wells, festivals on patronal days ("patterns") were all discouraged. The family Rosary, as part of evening devotions in the home, became common. The Synod of Maynooth, held in 1875, forbade the old system of home wakes, a custom which nevertheless continued. The funeral Mass, however, was moved to the church. Religious instruction, based on the catechism, brought a greater institutionalization of Catholic practices, and Catholic life was equated with obedience to concrete rules. Catholic theology and teachings were defensive and rigid, clearer than you could expect possible, especially moral theology with its list of categories, offenses, and laws of "how far" one might go in matters of sexual morality.

The worldwide background of this Irish church must be kept in mind. At this same time a great deal of centralization was also taking place in Rome. Pope Pius IX (1846–78) fought the loss of his temporal power, taken by Italy, by emphasizing his spiritual authority and pressing for the declaration of papal infallibility at the First Vatican Council (1869–70). A new devotion to the person of the pope soon became a part of Catholic identity and practice. The Irish had already been prone to this since the Reformation, since the pope represented an authority of more reliable standing to them than the Protestant sovereign of England. After Vatican I, they were even more faithful in their adherence to all that came from Rome. It is interesting to note that, at the First Vatican Council, 70 of the 700 attending bishops were Irish, and 140 were of Irish descent. Being Catholic, and perhaps more Catholic than anyone else, had become synonymous with being Irish, at least in the south of Ireland.

There is little of poetic value that comes from this period. As we shall see, whatever creative inspiration flourished at this time did not come from within the church. Though some of the clergy, as well as some of the people, favored movements toward national independence and native cultural expression, the majority stressed respectability and conformity in order to be accepted into the world of the Protestant ascendancy. Daniel O'Connell, acclaimed as "the Liberator" of the Irish, was quoted as having said in a moment of great exasperation:

> In times to come people will not give me due credit for the winning of Catholic emancipation, for it will not enter into the mind of man to conceive of what race of slaves I have to endeavour to make men.[12]

As a way to aid, support, and protect the many poor and uneducated people of the country, the church was growing into an authoritarian institution; it often used its power for the true well-being of the people but at other times used it in an abusive way. This system continued to function adequately for some time, at least until more people acquired some higher education. Meanwhile there were problems that had particular repercussions in the Irish psyche and spirituality.

Wine, Women, and Avarice

The main concerns for the clergy in this new church revolved around the issues of excessive drinking, sexual failings, and avarice. To some degree they were also the main issues of concern for all Catholics of this age. Drunkenness, even in priests, was usually accepted as human weakness and lust was likewise at least tolerated. But greed for money was, for most lay people, the most obnoxious sin of priests, and they would treat an avaricious priest with great disdain. There are many stories about clerical greed, and the old Celtic humor is not lacking. So one wag wrote that a raven will talk sooner than a priest lose his greed.

The Synod of Thules in 1852, in regulating how, where, and when a priest was to celebrate the sacraments, also dealt with the question of gifts and stipends. Money issues, including simony, had often been a concern with regard to poorly educated priests, as evidenced in the twelfth-century reforms.

More serious, perhaps, from the spiritual point of view was the question of the use and abuse of alcohol. There has been much discussion about the Irish propensity to drink. Some blame a genetic defect with deep Celtic roots. Certainly, beer and mead were part of the Celtic diet, as was wine for which they traded with other nations. Moreover, this was a warrior people with a love of exuberant living and wildness in dress, color, music, and song. Was there a propensity to manic-depressiveness involved in this? If so, then it is easier to understand how a defeated people faced with abject poverty would be inclined to addictive substances for escape. The famed Irish melancholy is also understandable as the natural result of hundreds of years of oppression. The famine was the dramatic and traumatic conclusion to a process of loss of land, loss of rights, and finally the loss of the ability to provide food for one's family, not to say anything of the loss of the possibility of sharing with others, as had been the practice.

There had been concern about the abuse of alcohol before the famine. The bishops' attempts to curtail the celebrations at holy wells, at pilgrimage sites, and on stational and pattern days stemmed from a desire to stop the abuse of alcohol. But whatever had been the previous history, there was a marked increase in the use of alcohol as escape after the famine. It began to shape the culture in a deeper way than before. To counter the drinking problem, parties and dances were discouraged and those which did take place were often chaperoned by priests. Temperance movements developed in the 1840s and became even stronger when the Pioneer Total Abstinence Association was founded by Father Cullen, SJ, in 1880, a group which flourished through the mid-twentieth century. The problem, however, continued as a feature of this traumatized people.

After the famine there was increased concern in the new church with sexual morality. In a lecture on the effects of the famine, University College Galway Professor Kevin Whelan claims that the Irish became more "puritanical, celibate, and docile."[13] The deep hurt and sadness that resulted from the famine experience no doubt disturbed the psyche and its natural expression. As men were unable to find work and the dignity of their manhood vanished they turned more and more to the bravado of the drinking culture. The women, weighed down by their own sadness and sense of failure, became the rescuers in this culture. This, in turn, had profound ramifications for the family, how children were treated, the place of sexuality and even of love. But the church moved in as the great guardian of sexual mores, created pressure to remain celibate, and prevailed on the Irish to get married at a later and later age.

This church pressure came partly from the influence of moral theology coming from the continent. But it may also have been a reaction to a population growth from 3 million in 1700 to 8.5 million in 1845 (and the population may have doubled between 1800 and 1845 alone). Was this an attempt to be responsible in curtailing the population? More study is needed to explain it all.

Also to be considered was the change in land ownership and farming. The old communal way was gone. Those who did manage to secure land now passed it on to the oldest son, who had to wait for mother to die and sisters to marry before getting married. Whatever the reasons, it is clear that the population never recovered its prefamine numbers. At least one million died and two million emigrated as an immediate result of the famine, and the population declined to between three and four million at the end of the century.

There was also an attitudinal change toward sexuality and a new shyness with regard to marriage. In the mid-eighteenth century girls were wont to marry before their twenty-first year. The census figures of the early nineteenth century show a marked tendency to even earlier marriage. Nor had celibacy ever been well accepted or implemented, even among the clergy. This all changed after the famine and a sense of guilt and shame began to surround sexuality. This was a dispirited people full of sadness, guilt, shame, and unfaced anger and grieving, a people unable to feed their own children. Add the abuse of alcohol and a negative attitude to sexuality and you have all the pieces for dysfunctional families.

Only recently have people of Irish descent been able to face not only the famine and its consequences but also remnants of it within themselves. Twentieth-century gender studies, first among women and then, more recently, in the "men's movement," have shed light on various cultural inadequacies and even maldevelopments of the sexes. The nineteenth-century Industrial Revolution brought changes to the roles of men and women throughout the West. Ireland was hardly part of the industrial world at that time, but the consequent arrival of the country into the twentieth century has brought its painful challenges. The Irish male has been characterized as having been emasculated by the destruction of his usual male role of working and providing protection and sustenance for his family and thus having lost his basic sense of self-worth. The Irish woman has emerged as the strength that held families together. When men were killed or went into exile or were spiritually defeated by the system, the women were left to raise their families on their own. Tom Murphy, a playwright from County Cork, writes in his introductory notes to the 1995 production of his play *Famine:*

> What about the other "poverties" that attend famine? A hungry and demoralized people becomes silent. People emigrate in great numbers and leave spaces that cannot be filled. Intelligence becomes cunning. There is a poverty of thought and expression. Womanhood becomes harsh. Love, tenderness, loyalty, generosity go out the door in the struggle for survival. Men fester in vicarious dreams of destruction. The natural exuberance and extravagance of youth is repressed.[14]

Men and women together became entangled in a systemic cycle of destructive behavior in marriages and families. The scenario has often played itself out in the picture of many an Irish family described to me both in spoken and written word. The husband is devoted to his mother and the wife takes second place. Children are born, and the mother showers her attention on them, which the husband resents. He then opts out by going to the pub for a pint, leaving the children to be raised by his wife. Her own maternal instinct prevents her from doing the same and even presses her into a martyr's position of nobly, but resentfully, carrying the family burdens. She resents being left alone and retaliates by with-drawing her love from her husband. Frustration, anger, loneliness, and depression all are part of this package. This negativity often causes the children to have a compromised relationship with the father, who is a very poor role model, especially for boys. Added to this picture is a lot of confusion about love and sexuality. A mother will sometimes transfer her suppressed love and affection onto her oldest son. This love, in turn, is of a conditional nature and given with the understanding that the son will never desert mother but will always be there for her. A variant expression of this is that he "give up his life" to the church as a priest, and still be tied to mother.

The cycle described above continues until at least one very en-lightened and strong person in the family through sheer hard work breaks the cycle of behavior. A change in this pattern has been occurring, thankfully, more frequently in recent times. The latter part of this century has seen a great awareness of these problems. The novels of John McGahern, particularly *Amongst Women,* have aptly described the emotional abuse of women. The well-acclaimed play of Brian Friel, *Dancing at Lughnasa,* sadly portrayed the plight of women and their victimization in rural Ireland in the 1940s. The poetry of Patrick Kavanagh, such as *God in Women,* has done the same. The wonderfully written memoir of Frank McCourt, *Angela's Ashes,* is a portrayal of the dysfunctional Irish family. This heart-wrenching story obviously touched many people and in 1996–97 the book was on the best-seller list. In 1992 a recording was re-leased in Ireland called *A Woman's Heart.* It consists of twelve songs sung by six well-known Irish female artists. All of the songs are about women's lives and difficulties. A year after it was re-leased the recording had outsold all recordings ever released in Ireland. One very poignant song is called "Sonny," which tells of a mother's love and need for her son. In the refrain she pleads with her son not to leave her alone, for her husband is a sailor and never comes home. The loneliness of both mother and son are drawn out in the verses.[15] Such painful sentiments are being acknowledged more and more in novels, songs, plays, and private conversations.

Irish-American Spirituality

The first wave of Irish immigrants to the new world occurred in prefamine times, in the early part of the nineteenth century. Many of them were Irish Protestants from the north, and they tended to settle in rural areas, maintaining the lifestyle they had left behind. Many settled in the southern states. There has not been much study done on these Irish, and it may be that they were much more easily assimilated than their Catholic cousins.

The new waves of Irish immigrants, after the famine, were quite different. They were mainly Catholics and they settled in urban areas. Except for their religion, which held them together in enclaves among often inhospitable natives, these new immigrants tended to turn their back on what lay behind — a rural, agrarian lifestyle and much that went with it. They arrived on the American scene at a fortuitous time when massive brute strength was needed to build cities, canals, and railroads. These newcomers, described as lazy and incapable by the English powers, now proved to be an industrious and hard-working people. Their assimilation into the American scene, into its politics and institutions, has been well documented.[16] Parallel stories can be told of Irish immigrants in Canada as well as in Australia and England itself. My concern here is more with their spirituality.

These Irish Catholic immigrants had left a very painful and horrific scene. Their journey over the sea on what were often known as "coffin ships" only added to the traumatic experience. Much denial would follow as a result of the need to forget and move on with a new life. In time, only pleasant, sometimes romantic, sometimes unreal memories would be passed on to the children. They would sing "Irish Eyes Are Smiling" but forget the many eyes that were sad and desperate. The celebrations of their ethnicity would revolve around shamrocks, leprechauns, cute stories, green beer, and great humor applied to everything, even the continued problem of alcoholism.[17] These new Americans entered the work force at the bottom. They often worked themselves into the police force and, apart from trades, tended to enter no professions other than politics and the priesthood. Many were, at first, illiterate, and a simplicity, sometimes tending to an anti-intellectualism, dominated for the first hundred years. Only in the 1950s did a good number of Irish-Americans enter the college and university world. Only in the 1970s did they show enough interest in Irish history, culture, literature, and art to justify and necessitate Irish Studies programs at various American universities.

The post-famine Irish came to a Protestant country. Catholics numbered only 5 percent of the population when they first arrived, but they would help to bring this number up to 12 percent within twenty years. In this process the Catholic Church would play a central role. The Irish lived in poor urban tenements and felt scorn and rejection from the populace around them. And so they coped by establishing strong neighborhoods built around their Irish Catholic identity. The parish church was the center of this neighborhood. It became normal for Irish-Americans to introduce themselves by the name of their parish, "I'm from Saint Kevin's." They soon built their churches, their schools, their hospitals and other Catholic institutions, paralleling those of the greater society. And in the center of all this was the priest. Many vocations came from their own midst and served their own people, but they also gradually became the mainstay of the entire American church. Irish bishops dominated the hierarchy. In the nineteenth century these church leaders were on the side of the poor and oppressed. They stood up for the rights of the worker, spoke out for the establishment of unions and proper working conditions. At the same time they were part of the Roman church that was becoming more and more centralized, buoying up the authority of pope, bishop, and priest everywhere.

The spirituality that this new Irish-American church exhibited was similar to that developing not only in Ireland but also in the entire post-Reformation church throughout Europe. It was similar to the spirituality being brought to the new world by other Catholic ethnic immigrant groups. It was characterized by a non-scriptural, non-liturgical, and non-mystical point of view. It was rather pietistic in its prayer forms, moralistic in its ethical approaches, legalistic in its basic approach to salvation. Novenas proliferated and served as a social, as well as spiritual, center for

Catholics. In pretelevision days and in a time when city streets were considered safe, crowds of people (mostly women) would come to evening novenas. They also attended Mass regularly and in great numbers, both women and men in higher proportions than among most ethnic groups. But the spiritual approach was passive. In a rather whimsical book called *Why Catholics Can't Sing,* the musicologist Thomas Day points to the Irish attitude to the Mass.[18] His thesis is that the Irish learned to be quiet and anonymous at Masses celebrated during the penal times when, in some circumstances, the Mass was celebrated in a way that the participants could not even recognize the celebrant. But there were other reasons for this too. Congregational singing, like the reading of scriptures, was considered Protestant (the same as being English). There were some songs for church use produced during this time, such as "Bring Flowers of the Fairest," "To Jesus Heart All Burning," "Mother at Your Feet Is Kneeling." Day shows that these are musically related to "Galway Bay," "My Wild Irish Rose," and "Sweet Rosie O'Grady" in style. These songs, he points out, are best sung by soloists and not by congregations. He sums up their content and style in the following observation:

> If you look at the words of these maudlin songs, which were associated for so long with "Irish-American" Catholicism..., you will notice that a few basic ideas keep returning: the congregation as a gathering of poor children, Mary as a source of consolation for the poor children, Jesus as the private savior for *me* alone, frailty, and weakness.[19]

Since the Irish influence was so strong in the formation of the nineteenth-century American church, another of Day's observations is interesting. He notes that an American of Italian extraction, two generations after Ellis Island, would visit Italy and be scandalized by "the way those people behave in church," but would visit Ireland and feel very much at home in the churches there. This was a triumphalistic church holding itself up above and against the forces of Protestantism, democracy, secularism, and the approach of the modern age. Papalism, a devotional fidelity to the pope, was part of this church. There were also many secondary characteristics of Catholicism that tended to divide Catholics from their fellow Americans to the neglect of the common Christian and more essential Trinitarian and Christological emphases on tolerance, openness, and unity. In this respect I refer to a devotional piety, laws and customs, and a spirit of separate structures and practices that marked a ghetto, albeit one of cultural unity rather than of a people segregated and forced apart.

Monica McGoldrick is a helpful resource for understanding the spirituality of the new Irish-American church, the way its members lived out their faith and beliefs and how it was deeply influenced by their history and by the famine in particular. In 1982 she wrote an intriguing contribution to a book about the various ethnic groups in America and the particular characteristics and problems, as well as strengths and insights, which each group brings to therapy and counseling.[20] While admitting that many observations appear to be stereotypical, the author claims they have been validated consistently in practice. She also notes that the types of behavior that she describes have been changing since the 1960s and the church renewal brought about by the Second Vatican Council (1962–65). We may infer that this is even more the case after almost another generation following her writing. But in sharing these observations with workshop participants I have found that many Irish-Americans, and certainly those in their middle age, respond with fascination when recognizing how accurately these observations describe their own experiences. Acknowledging them has also been an experience of healing and new freedom.

McGoldrick paints the Irish as a "paradoxical people": they are jovial, charming, and clannish when they unite but often have a sense of isolation, sadness, and tragedy. "The culture places great value on conformity and respectability, and yet the Irish tend toward eccentricity. Their history is full of rebels and fighters, and yet they tend to be compliant and accepting of authoritarian structures."[21] They are described, at least until recently, as plagued by guilt and rigidity. Poverty, the famine, a moral upbringing that stressed sin and guilt have all contributed to narrowness, intolerance, and self-righteousness. "Basic to the Irish character is the belief that people are bad and will suffer deservedly for their sins.

The myth of badness, related to the concept of original sin, is the unquestioned conviction that no matter how hard we try to be good, we will fail because it is human nature to be evil and be prone to sin." You cannot get any further removed from the old Celtic spirituality than this! The rigidity of the church is seen as contributing to all of this. And in this moral posture sex was considered to be extremely dangerous. "As a consequence of sexual repression, they also avoided tenderness, affection, and intimacy." For the Irish, marriage was often seen as permission to sin!

Another paradox is that the Irish are very verbal but fear speaking the truth because it will reveal how bad they are. This has led to an articulateness in most objective matters but an inability to express inner feelings. Anger is avoided as unacceptable, at least as directly expressed. "Except under the guise of wit, ridicule, sarcasm, or other indirect humorous expression, hostility in the family is generally dealt with by a silent building up of resentments, culminating in cutting off the relationship, often without a word."

Alcohol is the social substitute for food, possibly as a result of years of starvation. "While food provides Jews and Italians a major source of emotional solace and sharing, the Irish may at times be embarrassed to enjoy good food. The pub, rather than the family, became the center of Irish life." And the wife of an alcoholic is more likely "to seek support for her martyrdom than a change in her role or situation since a favorable change is beyond her expectations." Suffering in this spiritual worldview is deserved. One would become uncomfortable if things went well for very long. This does not mean that they seek suffering but that they expect it. In a wonderful passage from the German writer Heinrich Böll we see a fascinating comparison of Irish and German attitudes when something goes wrong:

> When something happens to you in Germany, when you miss a train, break a leg, go bankrupt, we say: it couldn't have been any worse; whatever happens is always the worst. With the Irish it is almost the opposite: if you break a leg, miss a train, go bankrupt they say: it could be worse. Instead of breaking a leg you might have broken your neck, instead of

a train you might have missed heaven, and instead of going bankrupt you might have lost your peace of mind.... And if you should die, well, you are rid of all your troubles, for to every penitent sinner the way is open to Heaven.... With us, it seems to me, when something happens, our sense of humor and imagination desert us; in Ireland that is just when they come into play.[22]

Other characteristics that McGoldrick notes include: the Irish emphasis on death and on celebrating death as the most important part of the life cycle; the domination of Irish women; fathers as shadowy or absent, usually avoiding their wives; a high regard for celibacy; discipline through ridicule, belittling, and shaming. The strongest axis in the Irish family is the mother-son relationship, probably because of the lack of closeness between parents. The mother idealizes her oldest son, sometimes not realistically. "This puts the son in a bind. Her underlying conviction is that men are weak and will let you down, yet she idealizes her son in a way that he cannot openly reject. But he knows he is not what she dreams of because indirectly she lets him know it."

When it comes to therapy, McGoldrick characterizes the Irish as shy in opening up, but willing to work because they are very loyal and willing to please. They can be helped, through their natural gift of word, to begin to communicate thoughts and feelings. And with their sense of responsibility and loyalty comes their greatest asset, a profound sense of humor. It is only now at the end of this twentieth century that Irish-Americans can look at their experience and apply their humor to it. This negative picture has come from pain and suffering. Even their sense of being Irish, McGoldrick says, was a sentimental part of their lives, and often they knew little of their heritage. Only now can Irish-Americans, and others as well, look at their heritage realistically and learn from it.

This chapter has explored "the darkest hour" of Celtic Christian history. As intended, the emphasis has been on much that was negative. The characterization of piety and spirituality in this way may offend some readers. By all means they should embrace what is helpful for them in their search for God and a fuller spiritual life. But the purpose of this description of the darkest hour has been to clearly distinguish it from an earlier "Celtic spirituality" and to understand how the change came about. "The truth will make you free," Jesus said. For those spiritual seekers who no longer find the spirituality of the post-Reformation church to be adequate, Celtic spirituality offers the opportunity to reclaim an older part of their own tradition. As Christians we believe in new life coming through death. And so in the midst of the darkest house there were also glimmers of light.

*Chapter
Seven*

Twilight or Dawn?

I SOUGHT TO UNDERSTAND what the ancient Celtic church was about and also how the more recent expression of Irish Catholicism came to be. After I found some answers to these queries, new questions emerged. The first was, Does anything remain of this Celtic church? Second, whether or not there are such remains, is the tradition, or at least part of it, worth retrieving for our own day?

In the last chapter I traced the decline of Celtic Christianity. Some consider this decline to be quite terminal. Celtic historian Peter Berresford Ellis sums up the arguments for this position in these words:

> By conquest, dispossession and the near destruction of their languages and culture, the Celtic communities have become severed from their traditions.... [They] have been separated from their forefathers by a deep cultural gulf, cast adrift among the accidents of translation. They have been told that the languages, culture and values they enshrine are anachronisms in the modern world. They are therefore becoming,

and indeed have become, gawky provincials in other cultures, not knowing their past, insecure in the present and uncertain of the future. The real heritage of the Celtic church, which their ancestors evolved and stubbornly defended through the early centuries of the Christian epoch, has not been passed on.[1]

I do not contest Ellis's scholarship. It is true that there is not any purely Celtic culture or nation now in existence. Nor is there a uniquely Celtic Christian church to be found anywhere, though it has evolved in diverse ways in the different Celtic countries. But I make a twofold contention. First, as indicated in chapter 1, I believe there are deep Celtic "fault-lines" that keep erupting after times of quiet repose and seeming death. Like the Jews, the Celts do not seem to ever fully disappear no matter what oppression and division they suffer. The existence of Ireland with its distinctive identity of Irishness is miraculous after centuries of a history that should have, in the normal course of events, meant extinction. At least one component in this Irish identity is the Celtic heritage and tradition. To some degree the same can be said of Wales and, to a still lesser degree, of Scotland, Brittany, the Isle of Man, and Cornwall. In this chapter I point out some ways this ancient tradition asserts itself, particularly in the area of spirituality. My second contention, which I will develop later, is that we who are about to enter the third millennium of Christianity can learn much from Celtic spirituality and appropriate some of its features.

Forging an Irish Identity

It was precisely at the very nadir of Irish history, the time of the penal laws and the famine, that the first stirrings of national identity and unity were felt. Ironically it was the Protestant Anglo-Irish who were the first to try to separate from England and to develop a separate identity and country. Such sentiments can be found in Jonathan Swift (1667–1745) and other eighteenth-century writers. When the Act of Union was implemented in 1801, many Catholics supported it believing that their lot with England would bring something better for them. They also believed that this union would be followed by Catholic emancipation since powers in England had often promised this. When emancipation finally came and the Irish Catholic Church emerged as a strong institution, then the Irish Protestants, particularly those in the north of Ireland, changed their minds about separation from England. The rise of the Orangemen followed.

Daniel O'Connell (1775–1847), great leader and orator, was responsible for the 1829 Act of Emancipation and had as his next goal the repeal of union. Circumstances, including the famine, prevented him from achieving his goal, but the momentum was gathering. The role of the Catholic Church in this movement to nationalism was often ambivalent. Tension between Irish Catholicism and nationalism went back to Wolfe Tone's rebellion in 1798, which touted a program based on French revolutionary ideas. The Vatican was a counterrevolutionary force in nineteenth-century Europe. Its influence was often used in support of English rule in Ireland. Open rebellion was condemned as hopeless, violent, and immoral. The Catholic hierarchy was divided on the question of Catholics going to national schools and on the need to repeal the Act of Union. Many of the lower clergy, on the other hand, were nationalistic in spirit and gave their support to rebellion, sometimes quite militantly.

Charles Stewart Parnell (1845–91) had some success in advancing the nationalistic movement, but he lost his moral base when he was involved in a divorce suit, which brought condemnation by the Catholic hierarchy. Other significant people of the age included James Stephens of the Fenian movement, which spawned the Irish Republican Brotherhood (IRB) in 1858 and the Fenian Brotherhood in America. Advocating the use of force, movement members were involved in uprisings in 1865 and 1867. On another front, Michael Davitt (1846–1906) founded the Land League in 1878, a popular movement using agitation, meetings, and social pressure to reacquire land for Irish peasants. All of this redefined and reasserted the peoples' identity and power. In 1842 Thomas

Davies founded the *Nation,* a newspaper of the "Young Ireland Movement," committed to justice for famine victims, rights of tenants, and a nation separate from England.

In England, Prime Minister William Gladstone attempted, first in 1885 and again in 1893, to get a Home Rule for Ireland bill through Parliament, but could not obtain the approval of the House of Lords. The Wyndham Act of 1903 did allow many Irish tenants to buy their own holdings. In 1912 a third Home Rule bill was introduced and again rejected by the Lords. There was hope of getting it passed in 1914, but it was then postponed because of the Great War. Modern Irish history begins with the Easter Rising of 1916, a heroic but ill-fated romantic rebellion led by a poet, Patrick Pearse (1879–1916), and drawing on Celtic mythology (Cuchulainn) and the Christian tradition (an uprising at Easter!). This was a typically Celtic undertaking: a great initial move backed by little reserves. And yet these revolutionaries were regarded as martyrs, raising the consciousness of their own people and that of the world — and the revolution moved on. A nation was born, a "terrible beauty" as Yeats would call it. English rule was shaken off but at the price of the division of the country and an ensuing civil war. The repercussions are still being played out today.

The Irish Literary and Cultural Revival

The reawakening of a distinct Irish national identity would depend on more than political parties, strategists, and militants. The race of Amergin, Patrick, Bridget, and Columban would also need poets, mystics, and artists. This literary heritage, though mainly oral, was never lost. In the hardest of penal times and famine pains, the people depended on their stories, poems, music, and dances to give them life and keep them going. Wherever the Irish language was still spoken, Celtic traditions of music, myth, and folklore survived.

But it was principally the Anglo-Irish Protestants, living in a world cut off from this living tradition, who would consciously return to the people's Celtic roots to reestablish an Irish national identity. These people had scant knowledge of the Celtic past, especially as we know it today. It is no surprise, therefore, that the return to the past was often a romanticized undertaking, a form of antiquarianism. The fruition of some of this work became known as the "Celtic Twilight," a last hurrah or celebration of a dead past. And yet their work was a contributing factor in the recognition of a heritage that could offer new insights for the present. Though much had been lost or buried, there was still "a list of doors that truth had left unlatched."[2]

The earliest indication we have of this conscious return to Celtic roots was, ironically, a forgery. When James Macpherson, in the 1760s, produced his Ossianic translations, he published them as the work of a third-century Celtic poet, Ossian. The negative reactions, some of which denied there ever was anything such as a Celtic civilization, sparked interest. The factuality of a real Celtic civilization soon came to light in the discovery of early artifacts of the Bronze Age. The Royal Irish Academy began its collection of Irish antiquities around 1840. Philologists, mainly Germans at first, began to study the Irish language in its Indo-European context. The ancient Brehon laws were published. Traditional Irish music was revived. Thomas Moore (1779–1852) wrote new lyrics in English based on old Irish songs, set to older Irish airs. Celtic myths, legends, and poems were edited and published, some of them for the first time in English.

Douglas Hyde (1860–1949), later to be the first president of the newly independent Ireland (1938–45), came from an Anglican family in County Roscommon. In 1893 he founded the Gaelic League, which had as its goal the "de-Anglicization" of Irish culture and the reassertion of the Irish language so that Ireland could live again as a distinct Celtic country. A man of many gifts, Hyde may best be remembered for *The Love Songs of Connacht,* a collection of songs and stories based on oral tradition and originally published in various journals. This work included love songs, drinking songs, songs in praise of women, various tales, and religious songs. They were published in both Irish and English. Although Hyde was trying to restore the Irish tongue, he unwittingly contributed to the recognition of "Hiberno-English," a very distinct kind of Irish-English dialect which would prevail in the literary revival.

Other nineteenth-century developments contributing to a nationalistic spirit include the founding of the Gaelic Athletic Association by Michael Cusack in 1885 to revive ancient games and sports, the National Literary Society in 1892, and the Abbey Theatre in 1899.

In 1881 Standish James O'Grady (1846–1915) wrote of the bards of Ireland. He sparked a desire to rediscover the heroic ideal in the mythology of Ireland. This example would be the inspiration of William Butler Yeats (1864–1939) and George Russell, known as Æ (1867–1935), who looked to Irish mythology and fairy stories for inspiration. And so interest in the ancient hero Cuchulainn was reawakened. With Lady Gregory (1852–1932), Yeats furthered Irish drama at the Abbey Theatre and mentored new playwrights such as John Millington Synge (1871–1909) and Sean O'Casey (1880–1964). Writers such as Samuel Beckett (1906–90), the poet Seamus Heaney (b. 1939), and playwright Brian Friel (b. 1929) contributed to the continuation of this literary renaissance. Today, Ireland continues to resound to the voices of many poets, such as Moya Cannon, Eavan Boland, and Nuala Ni Dhomhnaill.

The impact of these writers was summarized by Lorna Reynolds in a talk she gave at a Canadian conference on Celtic consciousness:

> That is what Yeats was himself attempting, what he wanted to encourage in others: the expression of that ancient idealism; the rediscovery of a mythology that by marrying the race to rock and hill would give it unity; the recovery also of the sense prevalent in ancient Ireland of the sacredness of the land, of every spring and stream, mountain and tree, of the indivisibility of all life, past and present, dead and living.[3]

At the same conference, Robert O'Driscoll spoke of the spiritual nature of the work of Yeats and Æ:

> Yeats and Æ cannot be dismissed as being involved in a kind of provincial primitivism, or of concerning themselves

with Celtic lore and legend in order to give their work local colour; what they deliberately set out to accomplish was to lay the spiritual and intellectual foundation of the modern Irish nation, to make what was instinctive, and on the point of being lost, part of conscious art.... At the root of the antagonism between Ireland and England... was the battle between two traditions, two ways of perceiving the world... between two civilizations, two ideals of life.... The Celtic Revival was deliberately created as a counter-movement to the materialism of the post-Darwinian age.[4]

Of somewhat different significance is James Joyce (1882–1941). Unlike Yeats and many of the Anglo-Irish, Joyce came from a Catholic background and brought a perspective from within the Catholic middle class. Joyce was concerned with the present, not the past, and Dublin, with its sights, sounds, and smells, was his favorite locale. He became intensely disgusted with the Catholic Church in Ireland for its censorship, for its narrow moralism and legalism, and for its episcopal control such as was exerted through a ban on Catholics attending Trinity College. Eventually he left Ireland in dismay, a modern Celt in exile. He settled in Italy but always with a backward glance to his beloved Ireland. His distinctive language has been described as a written form of the visual art of the Celtic knot and circle. His imagery is Celtic and Catholic. One of his last stories, "The Dead," is part of a compilation called *Dubliners*. It characterizes his view of Ireland as a dead society. The story takes place at an Epiphany party — epiphany being an image Joyce liked, an ancient Christian image of God breaking through the visible and ordinary. Despite his intense anticlericalism, his was a Celtic and Catholic sacramental consciousness. I think he may express what many Irish think of the church today and the innate spirituality that they still carry within themselves. I have always loved his description of what he thought the church really was, a parade of life in which "Here comes everybody!" I suspect he may well have had a more enduring influence on later Irish writers than many of the earlier "Celtic Twilight" literary figures.

A Spiritual Reclamation

The rebuilding of a national identity based on ancient Celtic roots included the recognition of the spiritual roots of this culture. The intertwining of the secular and spiritual components of life was ev-ident in the literary revival. The spiritual roots, so distinctive of the Celtic culture, lay imbedded especially in the language. The Irish tongue expressed an oral culture known for its imaginative perspective on life, death, and relationships within the whole of creation. This imagination influenced how English was spoken. This spiritual worldview was strengthened by the land, a mystical landscape touched closely by sea and sky. Despite all the changes, the Irish were a conservative people in speech and values and were yet to develop a truly urban culture. We are grateful to some en-terprising people for preserving some ancient treasures of this oral culture. There are two significant collections, one made in Ireland and the other in Scotland.

The Love Songs of Connacht, collected by Douglas Hyde, in-cluded a number of religious poems and prayers. These were published separately as *The Religious Songs of Connacht* in 1906. Some of these were quite old. Hyde refers to the fact that some poems of the thirteenth-century poet Donagha More O'Daly were still known and orally recited in the nineteenth century. The col-lection includes some traditional Catholic prayers and some stories of priests. Otherwise they are simple prayers for protection, for blessing of the ordinary events of life, prayers recognizing the place of saints such as Mary, Bridget, and Patrick in day-to-day living. Here are excerpts from a song called the "Bed Confession," found in County Mayo:

> May we lie down with God, and may God lie with us.
> A person from God with us.
> The two hands of God with us.
> The three Marys with us. God and Columcille with us.
> Is it not strong the fortress in which we are!
> Between Mary and her Son, Brigit and her mantle, Michael
>   and his shield,

God and His right hand, Going between us and every evil.
May we not lie down with evil, May evil not lie down with us.
The protection of the three Trees, the tree of the Cross, the
tree of the blood,
The tree on which Christ was hanged and from which He
rose again alive.
O King of the *cathair* [city] in heaven, Keep the spirit of my
soul from the real temptations of the adversary.[5]

There is a wonderful immediacy and intimacy in this prayer, a re-sounding echo of the ancient Celtic faith form, regardless of how ancient the prayer itself may be.

We have an even larger and more diversified collection of religious songs from the Scottish Highlands; there is no more precious collection of Celtic prayer than this. Alexander Carmichael (1832–1912), a speaker of Scottish Gaelic, came from near Oban in Scotland and worked for the Customs and Excise Department. From 1855 to 1899 he traveled over the western Highlands and islands of the Outer and Inner Hebrides, recording an enormous amount of material that existed only in oral form. One wonderful story he tells is of a man who gave him a poem and then walked twenty-five miles the next day to find Carmichael and beg him not to put it into print, for that would destroy its life! In Celtic cultures, as in many aboriginal cultures, the spoken word was precious. The collection first appeared in 1900 in two volumes of *Carmina Gadelica.* Three more volumes were published from his notes after his death in 1912. A comprehensive one-volume edition in English is now available.

In this wonderful collection of prayers, there is a variety of invocations, blessings, and supplications related to many aspects of human life: birth, baptism, lighting the fire, going on a journey, milking a cow, going to bed, commending a soul at death. They are direct and intimate. There is a great respect for the mystery of God in ordinary life. There is no question why a number of recent authors, such as Esther de Waal, have published these prayers in smaller collections with commentaries that allow one to savor them in a prayerful manner.[6]

Here are some excerpts from Carmichael's collection, one he calls "Joyous Death":

> Give Thou to me, O God, each food that is needful for my body;
> Give Thou to me, O God, each light that is needful for my mind;
> Give Thou to me, O God, each salve that is needful for my soul.
> Give Thou to me, O God, sincere repentance;
> Give Thou to me, O God, wholehearted repentance;
> Give Thou to me, O God, lasting repentance.
> Give Thou to me, O God, to confess the death of Christ;
> Give Thou to me, O God, to meditate the agony of Christ;
> Give Thou to me, O God, to make warm the love of Christ.
> O great God of the angels, bring Thou me to the dwelling of peace;
> O great God of the angels, preserve me from the evil of fairies;
> O great God of the angels, bathe me in the bathing of Thy pool.
> O great God of grace, give Thou to me the strong Spirit of powers;
> O great God of grace, give Thou to me the Spirit undying, everlasting;
> O great God of grace, give Thou to me the loving Spirit of the Lamb.[7]

This Celtic gift of soul has continued to endure in poetry, music, art, drama, and now in cinema as well. But the Celtic imagination is exhibited not only in professional and academic circles. It appears in pubs and parlors and even places of commerce. It is sensed in the tremendous revival of traditional Celtic music. It is apparent in Michael Quirk, a butcher in Sligo. From carving meat he turned to carving wooden sculptures of Irish mythological and historical heroes, retelling their stories as he carves them in your presence, enthralling all who watch and listen. Paula Murphy is another Sligo native who came to the United States for a while to study and work. But the land, its spirituality, and its poetry called her back to Ireland. Here is a poem on the Aran Islands which she shared with me:

Remembering soft rain and strains of tin whistle,
Silver sounds, silvery strains, plaintiff playing tin
I find myself seeking Him in the old mystical places,
In the wild flowers that bloom on Inishmor,* bloom by the
    stonewalls of Aran,
Honeysuckle, gentian, thistle, and haws.
I see Him moving as the wild grasses do by the sea, in the
    breeze, on Inishmor.
Purple-headed grasses swaying, tinged with violet, tinged
    with regret.

I see Him as the silver birch, the young oak among the tamed
    conifers.
I see Him as the black raven hiding in the green marble
    mountains of Connemara.
I see Him as the red deer, the silver wolf, on the side of Slieve
    na mban.*
Cloaked in mountain cloth,
Embroidered with golden and purple threads of gorse and
    heather;
Lovingly woven by the women of the Gael.

Inishmor is full of walled gardens where wild herbs grow:
Wild thyme, bittercress, and celandine.
My land is a walled garden perfumed by peat fires, bejeweled
    by their embers,
Filled with autumnal fruits: sloes, blackberries, rosehips, and
    elderberries.
As with the Druids of old, vanquished by the fruit of the
    Rowan Tree
These memories quicken me home.

---

*"Inishmor" = Big Island, one of the three Aran Islands.
*"Slieve na mban" = mountain of the woman.

Dun Aengus, stone fort, 1000–700 B.C.E., on Inishmor, Aran Islands.

Communal Efforts of Celtic Renewal

Many individuals thus exemplify the living Celtic spiritual tradition in their art, writing, music, and prayer. There are also some efforts being made to embody once again Celtic spirituality in communal and structural ways. One would hope that the churches would be glad to rediscover an older, richer tradition but this is frequently not the case. It is usually smaller, less institutionalized, groups that embrace their Celtic roots. One place in Ireland that has impressed me is the local pub. I have felt more spirituality in a pub than in some churches. Here one senses strong local community. In a pub one hears the old stories and songs, the tradition being handed down by the elders to the younger people, the history of the people with its joys and sorrows. You cannot remove God and spirituality from this tradition and history. Of course, there can always be a case of too much spirits in a pub, but you can also have too much religion in a church!

The Irish Catholic Church has been slow to change. It developed a tight identity that served the people in many fine ways after the trauma of the famine. But it was tied into a culture that was isolated from such developments as the Industrial Revolution and the ecumenical movements on the continent. Through the mid-twentieth century, a good number of the people remained poor and without much formal education. Three developments occurred in the post–World War II years to bring change to Ireland and to the Irish Catholic Church. A certain prosperity, accompanied by mass education, was the first. The second change was a certain mobility and openness to what was beyond the Irish culture. As tourism blossomed, foreigners started to come to Ireland in large numbers and many Irish people began to travel. The introduction of the national television service in the 1960s also helped to shatter the complacency of an insulated society. And finally a worldwide church revolution began with the Second Vatican Council. Whereas many Irish bishops were active in the First Vatican Council (1869–70), there was little contribution from the Irish at the 1962–65 council. Some believed that the Irish church was quite strong and adequate and the council was not needed in Ireland.[8] But the post-council years brought great change to Ireland. Many missionary priests and nuns in the 1970s and 1980s became involved with causes for oppressed people under neocolonial regimes and stressed Irish solidarity with small and poor nations. Vocations began to decrease in Ireland as they did throughout the Western world. Finally a number of events shook the church, beginning with the disclosure that Bishop Eamon Casey had fathered a son, and followed by the scandal of a number of priests charged with pedophilia. The secularism and pluralism of America and other Western countries took root on the Irish scene as well. Some decried the situation. Others saw it as an opening to a new, freer, healthier church. As elsewhere, the debate continues over whether the situation is getting better or worse.[9]

Individual church personnel have encouraged the Irish to find their Celtic Christian roots. Cardinal Thomas O'Fiach, late primate of Ireland, was a scholar who appreciated the Celtic tradition. He was fluent in the Irish language, a fine singer in the Gaelic tradition, and well versed in Celtic history and mythology. Unfortunately, some of his talks developing Celtic themes were criticized for seeming to challenge the English tradition of the church in northern Ireland and therefore for being unecumenical and popish. There are numerous other individuals, bishops, priests, nuns, and laity, who continue to turn to their Celtic Christian tradition in writings, in sermons, and in their work in local parishes and schools. Father John O'Donoghue is a poet and philosopher whose sensibilities are profoundly Celtic. The Redemptorist priest John J. O'Riordain has contributed much to the task of relating ancient Celtic Christianity and the present Irish church.[10] But these writers are far from being in the mainstream of the Irish church.

The church at Ballintubber Abbey in Mayo continues to be restored and functions as a parish church. It is also a center for many pilgrims arriving there, as well as for those setting out on Patrick's path to the holy mountain of Croagh Patrick, twenty-two miles in the distance. The chapter house has been opened as a meeting place and information center. A small museum park, Celtic Furrow, depicting the intersection of the original Celtic feasts (Samhain, Imbolc, Beltaine, and Lughnasa) with the Chris-

Gallarus Oratory, oldest completely surviving stone oratory from the seventh/eighth century, Dingle Peninsula, Co. Kerry.

tian church year has been built nearby. Three-day retreats on Celtic themes are also conducted there.[11]

At Glendalough in County Wicklow the national government has an orientation center with film, artifacts, and information about this monastic site. The site is enlivened by two priests (one Roman Catholic, the other Anglican) intent on once again making Glendalough a center of pilgrimage. It is a vivid experience in the Celtic vein of imagination and vision to join one of them in a day-long pilgrimage around the site, to stop and pray, to remember and feel what was once there, to find meaning and insight for today.

The Irish government preserves and makes available other Celtic Christian sites. While visiting the monastic city of Saint Ciaran at Clonmacnois, one can stop at the helpful interpretative center. Boats are available to go out to Skellig Michael, weather permitting, allowing one to spend time at the awesome monastic ruins on top of the rocky island. On the Dingle Peninsula one can visit many ancient "beehive" cells, the ancient Gallarus Oratory, and the more recently excavated small monastic remains at Riesk. These places of pilgrimage provide an opportunity to stop, to feel, to sense the place and its history and spirit.

At Ferns in County Wexford, Dominican nuns at Saint Aidan's Monastery have rebuilt three ancient hermitages of the eighth century: Cill Dara, Doire Cholmcille, and Cherith. Hermits are flourishing once again all over Ireland, possibly in reaction to the same kind of secularizing influence that once touched ancient Christian centers and drove Christians into the desert. Another very interesting development, paralleling such eremitic foundations, is the establishment of a Celtic-style monastery in Ireland by an American community. Father William MacNamara is a Carmelite priest and founder of the Spiritual Life Institute, a community of male and female "apostolic hermits" who have religious houses in Colorado and Nova Scotia. In 1995 they came to Ireland and started building Holy Hill Hermitage at Skreen in County Sligo. They believe their charism as apostolic hermits is in the best Celtic tradition. It will be interesting to see how well this group takes root and perhaps attracts vocations from the Irish populace.

It is not only in Ireland that Christian groups are looking to the Celtic tradition for new life. Though Scotland has largely lost its Celtic base, there are some places that give evidence of such a tradition. The Catholic Church in Scotland is much like the Irish and often has its base in Irish immigrants. The ecumenical community of Iona is alive as a praying, working, reflecting group sharing with the many people who come in pilgrimage to the island. Weekly all-day pilgrimages preserve the heritage of Columcille. The first Catholic presence on the island in four hundred years has come with the opening of Cnoc a' Chalmain (Hillock of the Dove), a Catholic house of prayer. Anglicans are represented with a retreat center, "Bishops House." The community at the abbey, though ecumenical, is under the Church of Scotland (Presbyterian). Elsewhere in Scotland, a Gaelic renaissance is flourishing in various places that stress the Celtic roots in language, history, culture, drama groups, and festivals. The Benedictine Abbey of Fort Augustus in the Highlands now offers residential Gaelic classes and monastic experiences for pilgrims as well. Dalraida, founded in 1986, is another Scottish group that promotes the Celtic culture, languages, and traditions. The Scottish Episcopal Church has a Gaelic society called Comunn Gaidhlig na h-Eaglais Easbaigich, which strives to raise consciousness about the church's Celtic background. In Wales, the site of Saint David's Cathedral remains a pilgrimage center for the Welsh in their search of an identity other than English. At the University of Wales campus in Lampeter, a master's program in Celtic spirituality is now available under the direction of Oliver Davies. Other specific Celtic programs are to be found at the Rowan Tree Centre in Powys, whose faculty includes Fiona Bowie and Esther de Waal, whose writings have done much to further a renewed interest in Celtic spirituality.

Many Irish-Americans are surprised to hear that there is considerable interest in Celtic Christianity in England. Many in the Anglican/Episcopal Church are searching for a spiritual identity in the pre-Reformation British church that had once been Celtic. Sometimes this is seen as a tradition within a larger tradition, that is, a British Celtic church within the universal catholic church. And sometimes it is seen as a contrast: the Celtic church of Britain as different from the Roman church, the community of John as distinguished from that of Peter.

There are also some intentional communities in England that strive to live within the Celtic tradition. One of these is the Northumbria Community centered at Nether Springs in Chatton, Northumberland. This group has also established a house near the tomb of Saint John in Turkey and a retreat house on Iona ("Duncraig") and is planning a house in Ireland. Another similar group is the Community of Aidan and Hilda, which is headquartered in Warwickshire. An American branch has begun under the name of the Community of Aidan and Bridget. Third, there is the center at Holy Island of Lindisfarne, once again a place of prayer and pilgrimage. A final place of note in England is Durham, where the tomb of Cuthbert invites reflection on the Celtic-Saxon church relationship.

In the United States there is a growing interest in Celtic history, literature, music, culture, and spirituality. For many people, the first step is the desire for a greater knowledge of their ethnic roots. Americans whose religious history has been largely voluntaristic tend to pick and choose individual ingredients that appeal to them. Religion and spirituality are mostly seen as private matters and often not associated with issues of culture. Harvard University has conducted a Celtic studies program for many years. There are numerous Irish studies programs at Catholic institutions, many established since the 1970s, for example, at Boston College, Stonehill College, and the University of Notre Dame. I have been discouraged that participants in these programs, according to conversations I have had with them, usually feel that spirituality as such does not enter their field of study.

One American group which promotes Celtic spirituality is called Anamchairde ("soul friends"). It is promoted as "a network for people committed to the Trinitarian faith, soul friends exploring Celtic Christian spirituality and the many gifts it offers to the church and the world today." The fellowship was begun in 1994 by five Episcopal men and women. Since then it has broadened its outreach to other Christians. It stimulates interest, awareness, and knowledge of the Celtic tradition through a quarterly newsletter, organized pilgrimages, and annual conferences.

Has Celtic Christianity passed into a twilight where we sense the last vestiges of an ancient tradition of the church? Or is it in the dawn of a new awakening to this heritage of wisdom for Christian peoples of today to understand and embrace? My own response to this query should be quite evident. I believe this is a rich Christian tradition that has much to offer us today.

Chapter
Eight

Contemporary Vision

PIRITUALITY, as I have tried to describe it in these pages, is the manner in which we humans face the transcendent in our lives, the particular way we approach the divine and ultimate reality beyond us. In the Christian tradition that also demands living fully open to all that is human. My final question in this study is whether the Celtic tradition is a spirituality for our time. On the eve of the twenty-first century will it enable us to move forward as more integrated Christians? Can it lead to a better world, to a better humanity?

I suspect that the answer will depend on one's basic approach to life, to God, to what it means to be religious or spiritual. If you begin with the conviction that the world, and the church with it, is going to ruin, then you might well believe the only hope is to return to past ways, to recover and restore the way we were. The emphasis then will be on a strong and closed identity and the need for rules and guidelines that are black and white in their clarity. I believe there are many who take this approach in our society and in the church today. It is manifested in a growing fundamentalism, in the appeal to a literal use of the Bible or a catechism or other church teachings. It is manifested in a nostalgia for the past, often for only the most recent past of the last century or, at most, the four-hundred-year period of the post-Reformation. This is called "tradition" by some, and they do not realize that this was an unusual time of the church marked by uniformity, little intellectual development, and a lack of appreciation of many earlier aspects of Christian tradition. Traditions such as Benedictine monasticism, centered on a strong paschal, liturgical, and biblical spirituality, are often not understood. Mysticism is suspect and considered even dangerous. Finally, this reaction is marked by a growing uniformity and centralization that, often for good motives, wishes to protect the integrity of doctrine and prevent people from losing their faith. Identity, an important value, is often overstressed out of fear of an openness that could dilute this faith.

There is another interpretation of our times that is possible. It often comes from the secular and scientific community which is aware of new insights into the cosmos. It is a belief that we are in a time of great transition, which is certainly bringing some confusion but not ruin or perdition. The cost of the transition, in this view, is some confusion and loss, but it needs to be endured in a spirit of hope in a future to which God calls us. In the Catholic Church this view was articulated in the 1960s by the Jesuit theologian Karl Rahner, who saw the Second Vatican Council as a great watershed in human and church history. It was his insight that this recent council was on the same level of importance as the First Council of Jerusalem (Acts of the Apostles, chapter 15). At that first council the infant church, impelled by the Holy Spirit, opted to move from being an exclusive Jewish church to one embracing all nations. That was not an easy change nor was it always successfully implemented. In a parallel fashion, the Second Vatican Council directed the church from being a European-centered church to becoming a truly universal church. This has brought problems of adaptation and inculturation; it has not been an easy adjustment nor has it been free from error. One might say that the church has finally moved out of its childhood stage into a stormy period of adolescence. Rahner foresaw that it would bring many difficulties, and he believed that future Christians would survive as such only by being mystics.

Another interpretation of the current transition comes from the theologian Ewert Cousins.[1] His thesis centers on the belief that the human race is going through a transformation that is bringing about a new global consciousness. Cousins begins with the work of the German philosopher Karl Jaspers, who, in a 1949 study, described a great "axial period" as having occurred between 800 and 200 B.C.E. This period gave birth to new movements in many areas of the globe: Confucianism in China; Hinduism and Buddhism in India; the Jewish prophets in Israel (whence would spring Christianity and Islam); Western philosophy in Greece. This effected a profound change in human consciousness: from being cosmic, collective, tribal, mythic, and ritualistic to being individualistic. This individual identity marks a consciousness that is self-reflective, analytic, and critical. In this transition some positive aspects, such as a connectedness with the earth and an interhuman dependency in community, were lost. The change led, however, to developments such as the spiritual search found in monasticism, the rise of individual moral responsibility, and the ascendancy of modern science and technology in the secular sphere.

It is Cousins's view that we are in the midst of a similar axial period and that a shift in human consciousness is occurring over the earth. This is a global consciousness that will bring communal and individual consciousness together. The view of the earth from the moon, the scientific understanding of the unity of all matter and energy, the growing openness of religions to learn from other spiritual traditions — all are signs of this transition. This new awareness is a reflection of a Trinitarian God in whom there is unity in differences. It is the promise of convergence from divergence. It is an image of great hope as we learn to see the present time of transition as one of growing pains toward a future that promises a deeper humanity, a cosmic unity of the universe — all a reality based in the Trinity. We will emerge from our present adolescent phase, but not until the present individual consciousness has run its course, not until we are tired out from the selfishness, greed, and violence that characterize it. I may not personally see it come, but I can help to bring it about. This is a vision of hope, and I believe we owe it to the next generation to hand on a spirituality that is open and hopeful.

In this time of transition, we turn to insights and awarenesses of our particular tradition that can help us move toward this new consciousness. The Celtic is one such tradition, particularly helpful for Christians. It is not the only one. Some learn from Buddhism with its spiritual practices of meditation and compassion. Others find an opening through feminist theology and the insights women bring from their experience. Some find a particular perspective, such as a creation-centered spirituality, through Native American culture or some new age approach. Some find their ground in medieval mystics such as Hildegard of Bingen and Meister Eckhart. Still others come to an enriched Christianity through distinctive church renewal experiences, whether charismatic, cursillo, or other small community and prayer support groups. There are many ways of convergence. These are ways for Christians to "come home" to their own Christian tradition when they are no longer nourished by the pietism of the past century and intuit the change of consciousness taking place. The Celtic tradition is only one of many such openings to a growing consciousness. But it is one that has been embodied in a definite historical Christian church (and is therefore not just an abstract ideology) and is also very modern in its appeal. It is not anti-intellectual but rather solidly based in scripture and tradition. It is rich in imagination and offers food for the soul encompassing poetry, music, the mystical, the body. It is also a communal tradition that offers an enrichment to the political expression of the church of the future.

A Lesson for the Church of Today

There are, then, two general areas in which Celtic spirituality influences us today. The first is the communal one of church structure and organization. The second is the personal spiritual approach it offers to individual believers.

As a communal form of the Christian church, the Celtic tradition offers an encouraging experience of inculturation within the larger universal church. It provides a definite image of how the kingdom of God came to be enfleshed in history and in a particular tradition for some centuries. This Celtic church was first, as we have seen, firmly built on local culture and respectful of local traditions. The Second Vatican Council brought back the concept of the local church, not as a lower department of the universal church, but as a concrete realization of the one universal church. It tried to balance the centralizing papal authority with the authority of local bishops and recognized the collegial nature of pope and bishops acting together. But this balance has not yet been achieved. A spirituality that emerged from the counter-Reformation made the pope a center of identity. People with this spirituality often see local bishops as minor players and the pope as the only true bishop. The richness of diversity, of local cultures, of local rites and customs has often been lost.

When we look at the church in earlier centuries we see a greater diversity. And the Celtic church, never fully part of Roman culture and civilization, especially preserved a sense of its own local identity. The spread of the early Christian church was, for the most part, tied into the Roman culture, to its form of government and curial office system. Christianity was acculturated into the Roman mindset. But Roman culture never came to Ireland, where Christianity was able to embrace and absorb an indigenous culture, bringing it to a new level of literacy, evangelical zeal, and holiness.

The Celtic tradition was very communal, expressing a horizontal equality and deemphasizing vertical, hierarchical differences. Men and women tended to be more equal than in the Roman experience. Clergy and laypeople were closer. The bishop was primarily an evangelizer leading his priests in works of spreading the gospel, but he remained a member of a local community of which an abbot was the administrative head. Together, the Christian community practiced (or aimed at practicing) a holistic spirituality that embraced the mind (respect for learning, preserving the tradition in writing), the heart (nature, poetry, music), and the body (penance and pilgrimage). It was a mystical spirituality that avoided later dualisms by seeing the sacred and the secular as one, the grace of God in the ordinary things of everyday life, the image of God the Creator in all of creation. It was definitely a worldview, a spiritual worldview that many people find inviting again today.

None of this is to imply that the Celtic church and the Roman church were two separate entities, nor do they have to be so today. The early Celtic Christians recognized and accepted the authority of Rome, though not subserviently. They rather trusted their own experience and respected their own particular gifts as worthy to share with a larger church. They were also able to live with paradoxes, differences (some more apparent than real), and not be discouraged by them. On the contrary we so often make things into a black-and-white, either-or, world. This is especially true in the church of today. While there have been many expressions of Christian spirituality in history, there are some who prefer one, monolithic spirituality as necessary for doctrinal unity. Some make a litmus test of loyalty and even of faith a particular expression of spirituality that emphasizes, e.g., an unthinking fidelity to the documents of the church magisterium, a stress on the real presence of Christ as the central focus of the Eucharist (over the sacrificial act of a community), or particular devotions to Mary.

Perhaps a metaphor would help here to portray how I see the possible relationship of such a worldview, the Celtic, conjoined with the universal church. I have found such a metaphor, a delightful one at that, in the writings of Rosemary Haughton. Her insightful work *The Catholic Thing*[2] was written almost twenty years ago but is helpful for us now. The author saw the need for a balanced view not only in the church of that time, but in Western culture as it was developing. To demonstrate this thesis, she sketched two allegorical figures. One is "Mother Church," whom she portrays as admirable, dedicated, most caring for her children, rich in experience, a good educator and guide, very talented in creating a good home for her children. But there is another side. The church also tends to feel that her will and God's are identical; her way is the best. Sometimes cynical, sometimes shrewd, she knows her children's limitations so well that she will not allow them to outgrow them. She will use her authority as she sees fit, "for their own good," even if that means being ruthless in suppressing revolt. She is suspicious of eccentricity and new ideas. Nonconformists are not well treated although after they are dead, she often feels differently about them. This is a Mother whom one may love much and yet fight against, one whom one may hate and yet respect.

But Mother Church has a twin sister, and her name is Sophia. She is often recognized by other names: Romantic Love, Mysticism, Superstition, Inspiration, Adventure, Imprudence, Sanctity, Folly. She has been an embarrassment to Mother Church, who has tried to keep her quiet or hidden although at times she realizes she needs her. And Sophia likewise has at times needed Mother Church to get her out of her muddles or sweep up the mess after her. In fact, if truth be told, each sister has admired the other. The same cannot always be said of their respective admirers, who often love one figure and hate the other.

Haughton implies later in her book that the Roman and Celtic church experiences are examples of this metaphor.[3] I think it helps to place them both in a light that lets us see that they are sometimes adversarial, sometimes in need of each other, often in a delicate but helpful relationship. As said more than once, the Celtic church no longer exists as such nor is there any question of resurrecting it. It probably carried the seeds of its own demise. Its dark side included a lack of discipline and recurrent bickering and fighting among its own members. The Celtic church needed the larger universal church. Perhaps if Augustine of Canterbury, Wilfrid of York, Margaret of Scotland, Bernard of Clairvaux, and others had been more sensitive to the mutual gifts of these traditions, the whole church might be better off today. But the Roman church has had its dark side too in its tendencies to use power to control and suppress and to close doors in fear that something new or unexplainable might emerge. It has often needed the Celtic adventurous and mystical bent in order to live more faith-fully.

The problem of inculturation of the faith continues today. For example, churches in Africa are in many ways similar to the primitive Celtic church. They might learn from the experience of the

Celtic church. Churches in Latin America are losing members to Pentecostal and other churches. Churches in Asia are beginning to face what being a minority religion means and how to interact with other more ancient spiritualities. The churches of Europe are struggling to stay alive as they witness the loss of members, a growing anticlericalism and secularism. Churches in North America and Australia have been European churches and their roots in an immigrant culture have not been deep enough to face up to the growing materialism, secularism, and consumerism of the times. The Celtic tradition seems surprisingly modern in its worldview and spirituality and appears to be one of the traditions in which modern people can find a contemporary Christian spirituality.

The church of today is more similar to the church of the fifth century than to that of many other eras. It is not like the apostolic church in which a few people began to permeate a larger society. It is not like the time of the spread of the early Roman church, which developed along with the larger culture. It is not like the church of the Middle Ages, which was a political as well as spiritual center of the world. Nor do the Reformation and post-Reformation spiritualities with their divisiveness, defensiveness, and triumphalism seem appropriate any longer. Today the culture largely ignores the real Christian tradition. In fact, at times, it is hostile and antagonistic to Christian claims. Western civilization is decaying as once the Roman empire did. A new type of Dark Age gathers around us. This was the scenario for the blossoming of the Celtic church. Might it not be the way again today?

A Personal Spirituality for Today

With a look now at what Celtic spirituality offers to a personal seeker, I can finally sum up what this Celtic Christian tradition is all about. It must be clear at this point that we are not speaking of a spirituality that represents a romantic escape from reality. To follow the spiritual worldview of the Celtic Christians is to embrace a way of life that is a real commitment to the belief that the Trinitarian God is alive in this world, that Christ remains incarnate in his church, that each Christian is called to active discipleship in building the kingdom of God. Celtic Christianity opens us up to a viewpoint that cannot separate Sunday and the rest of the week, this world and the next, the spiritual and the secular, the individual and the community. It would have great difficulty in understanding the privatization of religion that is now characteristic of Western culture and American life in particular.

To wish to learn from the Celtic Christian is to wish to sense the passionate presence of God in all of life. It is to find God in the ordinary events of life, love, eating, working, playing. It is to learn from the ancient saints, the medieval poets, the later prayers of the *Carmina Gadelica,* that everything is grace and blessing and we are to aim at bringing into consciousness the holiness of every moment. It is also to perceive that time and place do not separate us from what we ordinarily do not see and sense. The ancient Celts believed that the other world was always close to us and became apparent in the "thin times" and "thin places" in which the veil that usually obscured them was lifted. Yes, a wake and a funeral are such thin times and places, times to celebrate life as well as to mourn death. Mountains and wells are such places. But so is the hearth of a home.

The saints, who include all our ancestors, are also close to us and walk the journey with us. The doctrine of the communion of saints was a natural one for Celtic Christians to accept. We are not so much beggars in the presence of saints who, as it were, run bureaucratic offices to which we apply with prayers and novenas to obtain favors. They are, rather, friends with whom we dialogue, partners to whom we look for assistance on our journey. Intimacy and familiarity shared with close friends characterize our relationships with them. Jesus Christ is our hero, our sweet friend, as well as the local high king. He leads us into the life with his Father and shares his Spirit with us. The Trinity is reflected in many daily, earthy rituals that recognize the threefold dimension of all reality as touched by God. The Father is high king of heaven, a gentle and beneficent father, a wise and just ruler. The Spirit is a tangible comforter and protector. Protection indeed is necessary for there are also dark forces in the world, and evil is a reality not to be ignored. The church is our family in which we find assistance, support, and a sign of God's presence. Pope, bishops, and priests are brothers but never take the place of Christ, the Spirit, and the Father.

The God of the Celts is certainly God the "Other," a great mystery. This God is never to be reduced to the "man upstairs" or anyone we can capture and box in. And yet this wonderful, mysterious God is close to us, immanent in people and in all of the beautiful created universe. The earth is sacred, and we are part of it. The animal world helps us to understand ourselves as well as our God. In the natural world we also confront darkness, violence, and a sharing in our own need for complete redemption. The darkness and the emptiness, the pain and the grief, sometimes boredom and loneliness — these are all part of being human, and we have to face them in ourselves and in the world. Celtic monks sought out desert places, in fact, to face them more directly. But, despite its darkness, the world is still good. Humanity is essentially good. And our God is extremely good.

Because humanity is good, created by God, saved and redeemed by God, who embraces it in the flesh through the Incarnation, the body also is good. Human love and sexuality are good. The physical is part of spirituality because it is an essential part of our humanity. Prayer and love are expressed in the body — in fasts, in penances, in pushing ourselves to limits as disciplined athletes do. Pilgrimage remains an inviting spiritual phenomenon for two reasons. First of all, it engages the whole person, body as well as spirit. But it is also a social, communal undertaking. The purpose of a pilgrimage is not only to travel somewhere and get to one's destination. It is a journey on which one shares along the way. One shares one's bread, one's stories, one's faith and hope, one's love. One celebrates, along the way, the journey made by those who have gone before. The spectacle of thousands making the trek up Croagh Patrick or spending a weekend on Lough Derg makes me wonder if pilgrimage is not an underused spiritual tool in our times, especially inviting for the young and energetic.

The sense of the physical, finally, opens up the sacredness of place. Our own place is important, where we come from, where we belong, where we find God. Celtic monks sought the "place of their resurrection," that is, where they wished to die. Irish storytellers often recount what happened long ago as if it happened yesterday. Time is not important. But they always can tell you where it happened. Place is important. Do we not all have to find sacred places in our lives, even to become aware of the sacredness of our own house, our own garden, our own local church?

Celtic spirituality will not allow us to go it alone. It is never just between me and God. The community is important for that is where I know who I am. I also need particular people to share my journey in a special way. The *anamchara*, soul friend, is the one with whom I really come to know myself and my God. To come to know Jesus, Mary, and all the saints as my soul friends requires that I have a living human soul friend. The words of Saint John are appropriate here: how can I love God whom I do not see if I do not love those I do see?

Another spin-off of this communal spirituality is the prophetic role of the Christian. Celtic Christianity was a faith hammered out on the margins of Europe, on the margins of the known civilization, on the margins of the church. It was close to nature, to the elements, to God, and to homelessness, and often as well to poverty and starvation. The Celtic peoples have undergone oppression, suffering, and progressive marginalization. The mysticism that characterized the Celts is related to this. Only God was at the center and really important. All else was secondary. The seeking of material things and comfort could threaten this centrality. One must not forget one's own poverty, limitations, sufferings, and injustices. And from these one must reach out to the sufferings of others. Patrick never forgot the years he spent in slavery and loneliness, and he was the first European to speak out against slavery. Aidan, as bishop, chose a life of simplicity and care for the poor, giving away his horse and preferring to walk. Cuthbert, Columcille, and Bridget gave evidence of the same spirit. In our own days Mary Robinson, as president of Ireland, challenged the Irish not to forget the pain of the famine. But rather than turning inward to self-pity, she challenged them to reach out in empathy with peoples of the world, such as the Rwandans, people who suffer today as the Irish did in the past. A strong sense of social justice is a definite part of Celtic spirituality.

It is not only the physical and the fleshly that are important for the spiritual life. The mind is also a human gift to be nourished and developed. Knowledge should never be an impediment to faith. The preservation of learning, religious and secular, was important to the monastic copyists. The Bible, in particular, was honored by its artful editions as well as its place in the prayer, reading, and study of Celtic Christians. Monasteries were the schools of the times, even the universities of their time, with thousands of students from all over Europe. Columban and Scotus Eriugena were but two of the many Celtic theologians. So too a Christian today needs to read, study, be informed.

Scripture, especially the psalms, was the heart of Celtic prayer. "Mountains jumping like lambs" and "rivers clapping their hands" are expressive images in the psalms, and this imaginative approach appealed to the Celts. A fundamentalist understanding of the scriptures would never be natural to them. No more would a strictly literal and fundamentalist reading of the scriptures appeal to them than would a moralistic and legalistic approach to keeping the commandments. Both required life, spirit, imagination, and passion. And the Celts had plenty of these! In addition to logic and reason, poetry, song, art, and beauty were tools of knowledge. Our own culture seems to have trouble with this balance. We tend to be abstract and conceptual in our overdeveloped intellectual approach to knowledge. Or others prefer shallow slogans and easy formulas in an overdeveloped emotionalism. The Celtic mind was attracted to symbols, metaphors, visual and oral images, to the use of the senses, to icons and high crosses, illuminated manuscripts, metalwork, to a music that was deeply rhythmic and mantric, to dreams, poetry, and drama. To follow the Celtic spiritual way we modern Christians will have to do a lot of "soulwork" to develop our unused imagination, our neglected senses, to complement our rational minds.

In summary, prayer needs to be not just part of us but all of us. We need to pray with the whole of ourselves, my full person in harmony with all creation, not just with words but going beyond words, using heart, images, and body. This tradition is a call to return to our roots in the clay of the earth from which we come and to the Spirit of God in whom we dwell. If we can do this, we will find our prayer is our life and our life is our prayer.

Celtic Christianity: A Choice

There are many spiritual paths to follow in order to pursue the absolute, the transcendent, the divine. And there are many expressions of the spiritual path within Christianity without prejudice to a common belief in a Trinitarian God, an Incarnate Christ, and a community of church. Catholicism, which so often has seemed monolithic to those both within and outside its body of adherents, has a richness of diverse traditions. The various religious orders have each had a particular spiritual emphasis, and this includes Franciscans, Carmelites, Benedictines, and a host of others. Catholics have had a mystical bent or an apostolic bent or a combination of both. Some have emphasized Mary as the main focus of prayer and piety. Later forms of spirituality were more devotional and pietistic. Spiritualities have been affected by cultural factors such as Puritanism and the dualisms of the Enlightenment, and by historical factors such as plagues, crusades, and famines.

In our study we have looked at the particular spiritual approach of the ancient Celts, the way they saw the world, themselves, and the beyond. We looked at how Patrick and Christianity absorbed this worldview in a Celtic Christian expression, building on the culture but transforming it through the Christian sacramental worldview. Then we saw how it changed in medieval times because of both internal and external circumstances. The manifestation of much of the spirituality of the churches in Celtic countries in the twentieth century has had little to do with the old ways. But we also witnessed the preservation of some of this spirituality in the people, their language, their cultural ways of poetry and music, and in the very land itself. Many are turning to this type of spirituality again as an approach that seems consistent with our more universal view of the world and cosmos, with the understanding of ourselves acquired through contact with other influences such as religious traditions of the East. It is providing many with a way to view God and the world that is more unifying and balanced. Noel Dermot O'Donoghue claims that Celtic spirituality is threefold (what else!): ascetic, mystical, and visionary. It is a way not so much of doing things as of seeing things. It is a way to see God, Christ, church, prayer, morality, ritual, humanity, the world in a richer and deeper way than many of us have previously experienced.

Since Celtic spirituality is principally a way of seeing, sensing, and understanding, it can be adapted to our own lives today. Some practices common to the ancient Celts might not be appropriate today; the extreme penances might be an example. Some later developments may be taken on even though they were not part of early Celtic Christianity, such as daily Mass or the Rosary, for those who treasure these spiritual tools. There is a good deal of latitude within the common tradition. Some, I believe, will find they are between spiritualities. Much of what has been described as Celtic spirituality will appeal to them. But they will also find that they are still attracted to old pieties, old prayers and practices, that they learned as children. Occasionally the two traditions will clash.

I believe it is very natural to look back at the faith we had as children and consider it as normative, "what ought to be." We might remember a warmth, security, and protectiveness in our relation both to parents and to God. Some feel they have lost their faith because they no longer feel that way. But what is missed here is the opportunity to grow in faith. Real faith development means change, conversion, transformation. It means a deeper expression of what our humanity is about so that it truly reflects the image of God. This can be found only by going forward, sometimes through darkness, always in faith and prayer. The paradox then shines through, especially as we look at some of our spiritual elders who have gone this way. They do indeed manifest the simplicity, innocence, and security of a child that comes from simple faith. But now this faith has been proven and found worthy. The spiritual journey requires work and commitment. The Celtic way has shown how this might be done.

I grew up, like many of my contemporaries, in a "Catholic culture" that was coherent and unified. Once even partially shattered, the whole edifice became weak and vulnerable. For some the old culture still works, and they are determined to hold on to it. Others of us agree that Western culture and Western spirituality have been notable accomplishments but now regard them as inadequate. We in the West have developed a spirituality that has been very psychological and individualistic, pragmatic and action oriented. A notable contribution of the modern church has been in the active and moral sphere. It has been the voice of the poor, the oppressed, the unborn, the homeless, the emigrant refugee. But Western spirituality has lacked the mystical spirituality of an earlier church. I believe the Celtic church tradition shares more with the Eastern church and its spirituality than with much that is Western.[4]

Western theology has often been accused of an overdevelopment of Christology to the neglect of the Holy Spirit and of the entire Trinity as community and relationship. Eastern theology has emphasized the Trinitarian dimensions of all spirituality. It has also emphasized mysticism and contemplative prayer. It has believed in the goodness of creation and rejected the dualistic separation of natural and supernatural, creation and grace. Unlike the West of today, it has embraced the need for asceticism and compunction as central to prayer life. The Celtic approach is in harmony with this type of spirituality. I believe this is what many people are seeking in many places and often miss it in their own Christian tradition.

Our survey of the Celtic tradition closes with a prayer attributed to the sixth-century Irish monk Saint Ciaran, although it is likely that it was actually composed a century or two later. The first line is in Latin and the rest of it is in Irish, translated by Oliver Davies in his anthology.[5] The Latin line is from the psalms, exemplifying the ancient view that our prayer must be based on the scriptures and all our prayer should be a response to God's word. The remainder of the prayer is in the form of a litany, one of the many litanies of repentance of the time. Repentance, sorrow for sin, was a common theme of prayer. Acknowledging the need for redemption as well as celebrating the joys of creation were balanced in Celtic thought. The litany is a form of prayer of cadences and repetitions, mantric in form. The force of repetition, of saying something over and over, mirrors the waves of the sea constantly coming in and washing over us, cleansing and purifying us.

The prayer is full of images. God is portrayed as storyteller, as warrior, as the sun and sea themselves. This is a cosmic vision. Though it is a prayer of penance, there is no mention of sin, the sinner, guilt, or shame. There is no self-absorption, no psychologizing. Rather it is totally God-centered, affirming God's love and the grandeur of the giver of gifts. This type of prayer was probably prayed in the cross-vigil position, that is, with arms extended horizontally in the form of the cross. That brought in the physicality of prayer. You don't pray just in the mind but with all your soul and strength. In summary, this is a prayer that is truly Celtic in inspiration and Christian in content:

"According to the multitude of your mercies, cleanse my
   iniquity." (Psalm 51)

O star-like sun, O guiding light, O home of the planets,
O fiery-maned and marvelous one, O fertile, undulating, fiery
   sea,
   Forgive.
O fiery glow, O fiery flame of Judgment,
   Forgive.
O holy storyteller, holy scholar, O full of holy grace, of holy
   strength,
O overflowing, loving silent one, O generous and thunderous
   giver of gifts,
   Forgive.
O rock-like warrior of a hundred hosts,
O fair-crowned one, O victorious, skilled in battle,
   Forgive.

Notes

Chapter One: Ancient Celts and Modern Christians

1. It is pronounced with a hard *K* sound. When the word was transliterated into Latin, it became Celta, pronounced with a hard S sound in classical Latin but with a soft S sound in ecclesiastical Italianized Latin.

2. Thus the Irish word for mother, *mathair,* is related to *mater, mère,* and *madre* in Latin, French, and Italian.

3. Dora Jane Hamblin, "Once Maligned, Celts Are Now Touted as the First Europeans," *Smithsonian* 24, no. 2 (May 1993): 118–25.

4. Similarly it was Greece more than Rome that influenced Celtic philosophy, ideas, and mysticism.

5. The shrieking and yelling of bards as warriors went into battle was supposedly taken up in the practice of the many Irish-American soldiers in the American Civil War, who marked their opening salvos with their "Johnny Rebel" cries.

6. This respect for the head as the place of the soul of a person (what we would call the heart of a person) can also be seen in heads on sculptures and even on later Christian buildings.

7. When visiting the Blasket Islands off the west coast of Kerry in Ireland I was interested to hear that when the last inhabitants were evacuated in 1953 there was still a "king" recognized on the main island, witnessing to how this ancient understanding of local kingship had endured.

8. Peter Berresford Ellis, *Celtic Women: Women in Celtic Society and Literature* (Grand Rapids: Wm. B. Eerdmans, 1996).

9. "Ireland is a Mediterranean country surrounded by Anglo-Saxons" is one way the reality has been expressed.

10. An American branch of the league was formed in 1974.

11. A Welsh television station has helped to revive the popular use of the language. A similar development has more recently also occurred in Ireland.

12. In 1996 the creative Irish musical group "The Chieftains" recorded an album of Galician music, entitled *Santiago,* New York: MMG Classics (RCA Victor).

Chapter Two: Christianity Comes to the Celts

1. "Shape-shifting" refers to the recurring phenomenon of a person changing into an animal or other form. We find it, for instance, in the story of Finn

MacCumhaill, and it appears in the story of Saint Patrick, who became a deer when sought by the king's warriors.

2. Nora Chadwick, *The Celts* (London: Penguin Books, 1971). See especially chap. 7, "Christianity."

3. Ray Simpson, *Exploring Celtic Spirituality* (London: Hodder and Stoughton, 1995), 27–33, "John and the Eastern Connection."

4. This is a pre-Augustinian theology not yet preoccupied with sin and redemption.

5. A helpful reflection on Celtic theology and spirituality of place can be found in Philip Sheldrake, *Living between Worlds: Place and Journey in Celtic Spirituality* (Boston: Cowley Publications, 1995).

6. Leeks have since become the national emblem of Wales.

7. Arwel Hughes, *Dewi Sant: An Oratorio Sung in English* 1990. Copyright © Aureus Publishing Co., Cardiff, Wales. Quoted with permission of Meuryn Hughes (grandson of composer) of Aureus Publishing.

8. All quotations are from Saint Patrick's "Confession" as translated from the Latin, with commentary by Liam De Paor, in *Saint Patrick's World: The Christian Culture of Ireland's Apostolic Age* (Dublin: Four Courts Press, and Notre Dame, Ind.: University of Notre Dame Press, 1993).

9. This has been the cause of much conjecture. Our minds today might suspect some sexual failing, but it has been thought it could even have been some form of homicide.

10. De Paor, *Saint Patrick's World*, 98.

11. Ibid., 99, 108.

Chapter Three: Celtic Monasticism

1. The word "monk" comes from the Greek *monos*, which can refer to oneness, aloneness. This can mean either the single focused concern of the person for one thing alone, God, or perhaps the centering on the One which is God.

2. Some, in fact, think he went to the island monastery of Lerins while in France.

3. This is called "kenosis" from the Greek word for self-emptying as found in Paul's letter to the Philippians, 2:6–7: "...though he was in the form of God, [Christ] did not regard equality with God something to be exploited, but emptied himself, taking the form of a slave."

4. Delightfully related in Thomas Cahill, *How The Irish Saved Civilization: The Untold Story of Ireland's Heroic Role from the Fall of Rome to the Rise of Medieval Europe* (New York: Doubleday, 1995), 246.

5. Jean Markale, *The Celts: Uncovering the Mythic and Historic Origins of Western Culture* (Rochester, Vt.: Inner Traditions, 1993).

6. The site of the actual monastery is now the site of an Anglican

cathedral, originally built in 1229, and a high round tower from the ninth century.

7. Fr. Colm Kilcoyne, as quoted in Michael J. Farrell, "Feisty New Ireland Leaves the Church Panting to Keep Up," in *National Catholic Reporter* 30, no. 35 (July 29, 1994): 9.

8. "Cogitosus's Life of St. Bridgid the Virgin," in Liam De Paor, trans. and ed., *Saint Patrick's World: The Christian Culture of Ireland's Apostolic Age* (Dublin: Four Courts Press, and Notre Dame, Ind.: University of Notre Dame Press, 1993), 223–24.

9. De Paor makes this conjecture in ibid., 49, while lamenting the scarcity of adequate sources.

10. In recent years this site has once again been the terminus of regular pilgrimages as the local people pray and walk together to the summit.

11. It was from this site that Tim Severin set forth in 1976 on his boat *The Brandon,* to retrace the journey Brendan is said to have made across the Atlantic.

12. Des Lavelle, *The Skellig Story: Ancient Monastic Outpost* (Dublin: O'Brien Press, 1993).

13. Bob Willoughby, trans., *Voices from Ancient Ireland* (London: Pan Books, 1981).

14. Peter O'Dwyer, OCarm, *Towards a History of Irish Spirituality* (Dublin: Columba Press, 1995), 23.

15. The historical development of the sacrament is somewhat complicated. However, the early experience of penance as a "second plank" after baptism evolved in Rome principally for serious sins for which public penance was demanded. The Irish experience took this sacrament in a new direction.

16. From a letter to Pope Boniface IV, 613 c.e., as in De Paor, *Saint Patrick's World,* 141.

17. Nora Chadwick, *The Age of the Saints of the Early Celtic Church* (London: Oxford University Press, 1961), 90.

Chapter Four: Crises and Continuation

1. Arianism, for example, denied the divinity of Christ. It was refuted at the Council of Nicea in 325.

2. See M. Forthomme Nicholson, "Celtic Theology: Pelagius," in James P. Mackey, ed., *An Introduction to Celtic Christianity* (Edinburgh: T. & T. Clark, 1989), 413.

3. Ibid., 412.

4. At that time, the word "Scot," as in the name John Scotus, actually meant Irishman. The name goes back to "Scotta," the name of the mother of the Milesian invader of Ireland. Later, as many Irish settled in Alba, the name became the title for the local people, known to us as the Scots of Scotland.

5. See especially the introduction to Christopher Bamford, *The Voice of the Eagle: The Heart of Celtic Christianity: Homily on the Prologue to the Gospel of St. John by John Scotus Eriugena* (Hudson, N.Y.: Lindisfarne Press, 1990).

6. Britain, of course, already had Celtic roots. For example, even the city of London has a Celtic name, Lugdenensis, named in honor of the god Lugh.

7. See Clifford Stevens, "Saint Cuthbert: Crisis In Northumbria" in *Cistercian Studies Quarterly* 24 (1989): 280–92. This article gives a good historical background to the Whitby affair.

8. John J. O'Riordain, CSSR, *Irish Catholics: Tradition and Transition* (Dublin: Veritas Publications, 1980), 36.

9. Translation from the Irish by Bob Willoughby, *Voices from Ancient Ireland* (London: Pan Books, 1981).

10. The original manuscript of this poem was found in the monastery of Saint Paul, Unterdrauberg, Carinthia, which is now modern Slovenia. It seems it was written by an Irish scribe studying abroad.

11. N. D. O'Donoghue, "St. Patrick's Breastplate," in Mackey, *An Introduction to Celtic Christianity*, 60. The translation of the Breastplate, as above, is also a reworked rendition done by O'Donoghue of an older traditional translation.

12. See especially Maire and Liam De Paor, *Early Christian Ireland* (London: Thames and Hudson, 1958), chap. 5, "The Vikings," 131–60.

13. Historians dispute whether the Irish were really united against the Vikings or whether rival Irish kings were not actually more interested in curbing Brian Boru and the ambitions of his Dal Cais clan from Clare.

14. Jacqueline O'Brien and Peter Harbison, *Ancient Ireland: From Prehistory to the Middle Ages* (London: Weidenfeld & Nicolson, 1996), 78.

15. Ibid., 80.

16. Some of these towers can be climbed. After paying my fee of an Irish pound, I was able to get to the top of the tower at Saint Bridget's Cathedral in Kildare, there to view the beautiful countryside.

Chapter Five: Decline

1. Most of the eleventh-century bishops of Dublin were Irish Benedictines. This practice of episcopal consecration in England may have grounded the image of Benedictines as a part of the English church.

2. St. Bernard, *Life of St. Malachy*, trans. A. Luddy (Kalamazoo, Mich.: Cistercian Publications, 1978), 135.

3. John J. O'Riordain, CSSR, *Irish Catholics: Tradition and Transition* (Dublin: Veritas Publications, 1980), 31.

4. Benedictine monks had already come from the continent to Ireland, possibly as early as the tenth century.

5. Maire and Liam De Paor, *Early Christian Ireland* (London: Thames and Hudson, 1958), 175.

6. Ibid., 183.

7. Jacqueline O'Brien and Peter Harbison, *Ancient Ireland: From Prehistory to the Middle Ages* (London: Weidenfeld & Nicolson, 1996), 149.

8. This group was different from the Augustinian Canons Regular, more similar to the Cistercians in lifestyle, whom Saint Malachy had brought a century earlier.

9. Louis McRedmond, "The Friars in Ireland: The First Century," a talk given at Gort Muire, Dublin, reprinted in *Religious Life Review* (Dublin) 35, no. 176 (January–February 1996): 20–21.

10. Anthony Duncan, *The Elements of Celtic Christianity* (Rockport, Mass.: Element Books, 1992), 81.

Chapter Six: The Darkest Hour

1. These numbers are taken from Peter Berresford Ellis, *Hell or Connaught: The Cromwellian Colonisation of Ireland* (Belfast: Blackstaff Press, 1988).

2. Attributed to Gratianus Lucius in 1662, quoted in John J. O'Riordain, CSSR, *Irish Catholics: Tradition and Transition* (Dublin: Veritas Publications, 1980), 49.

3. Jacqueline O'Brien and Peter Harbison, *Ancient Ireland: From Prehistory to the Middle Ages* (London: Weidenfeld & Nicolson, 1996), 226.

4. See Kevin Whelan (Professor of History at University College Galway), "Bitter Harvest," a lecture given at Boston College, reprinted in *Boston College Magazine* (Chestnut Hill, Mass.) 55, no. 1 (Winter 1996): 20–25.

5. Seamus Deane, "Famine Politics," in *Irish-America Magazine*, New York (November–December 1996): 56.

6. O'Riordain, *Irish Catholics*, 64.

7. The scene is portrayed in Peter O'Dwyer, OCarm, *Towards a History of Irish Spirituality* (Dublin: Columba Press, 1995), 221–50.

8. See Patrick J. Corish, *Maynooth College 1795–1995* (London: Gill and Macmillan, 1996).

9. "Read the Mass" is itself an interesting expression connoting a mechanistic and ritualistic approach, as distinct from one that focuses on celebration, offering sacrifice, or presiding.

10. O'Riordain, *Irish Catholics*, 69–70.

11. "Making nine first Fridays," i.e., to go to Confession and receive Holy Communion on the first Friday of nine consecutive months.

12. See O'Riordain, *Irish Catholics*, 65.

13. Forum on the Irish Famine, Boston College, December 10, 1996.

14. Tom Murphy, *Famine*, presented by the Sugan Theatre Company, Boston Center for the Arts, February 23–March 11, 1995. Program notes from the playwright.

15. "Sonny," attributed to R. Hynes, on *A Woman's Heart* (Dublin: Darte, marketed by Dolphin Traders, 1992).

16. See, for instance, Andrew Greeley, *The Irish Americans: The Rise to Money and Power* (New York: Harper and Row, 1981).

17. Until recently, Hallmark and other greeting card makers have indulged in exploiting the "cuteness" of Irish drinking in their Saint Patrick's Day cards. Such stereotypes are now considered unacceptable.

18. Thomas Day, *Why Catholics Can't Sing: The Culture of Catholicism and the Triumph of Bad Taste* (New York: Crossword, 1990). See especially chap. 2: "The Irish Way," 18–34.

19. Ibid., 29.

20. Monica McGoldrick, John K. Pearce, and Joseph Giordano, *Ethnicity and Family Therapy* (New York: Guildford Press, 1982), especially chap. 15: "Irish Families" by Monica McGoldrick, 310–39. A second edition of this book appeared in 1997. The latter covers many more ethnic groups but many of the chapters, including the one on the Irish, have been reduced in size and coverage.

21. Ibid., 311. Succeeding quotations are from this source.

22. Heinrich Böll, "Irish Journal," 1967, in McGoldrick, "Irish Families," 320.

Chapter Seven: Twilight or Dawn?

1. Peter Berresford Ellis, *Celtic Inheritance* (London: Constable and Co., 1992), 156.

2. An expression used by Patrick Kavanagh in his poem "In Memory of My Mother."

3. Lorna Reynolds, "The Irish Literary Revival: Preparation and Personalities," in Robert O'Driscoll, ed., *The Celtic Consciousness* (New York: George Braziller, 1981), 393, 395.

4. Robert O'Driscoll, "The Aesthetic and Intellectual Foundations of the Celtic Literary Revival in Ireland," in O'Driscoll, *The Celtic Consciousness*, 403, 407.

5. Oliver Davies and Fiona Bowie, *Celtic Christian Spirituality: An Anthology of Medieval and Modern Sources* (New York: Continuum Publishing Co., 1995), 158. Copyright by Oliver Davies and Fiona Bowie. Reprinted with permission of the Continuum Publishing Company.

6. See de Waal's books, *The Celtic Vision, Every Earthly Blessing, God under My Roof, The Celtic Way of Prayer*; see also Noragh Jones, *Power of Raven, Wisdom of Serpent*, a collection of these prayers selected especially for women.

7. Alexander Carmichael, *Carmina Gadelica: Hymns and Incantations* (Hudson, N.Y.: Lindisfarne Books, 1994), 687 pp.; see poem no. 348, pp. 314–15. Used by permission of Lindisfarne Books.

8. In the years immediately following the council, Desmond Fennell was the Dublin editor for the German journal *Herder Correspondence* and sent reports in on the Irish church situation. With further editing some of these have been gathered in a book that provides interesting insights into these years. See Desmond Fennell, ed., *The Changing Face of Catholic Ireland*, foreword by Karl Rahner, SJ (Washington, D.C.: Corpus Books, 1968).

9. An interesting set of essays exploring this issue is Sean MacReamoinn, ed., *The Church in a New Ireland* (Dublin: Columba Press, 1996).

10. In addition to his fine book previously quoted, *Irish Catholics: Tradition and Transition* (Dublin: Veritas Publications, 1980), John J. O'Riordain, CSSR, has more recently written *The Music of What Happens: Celtic Spirituality, A View from the Inside* (Dublin: Columba Press, 1996).

11. At present writing these are conducted by Father Frank Fahy and Sister Maureen Gallagher, RSM.

Chapter Eight: Contemporary Vision

1. Ewert Cousins, *Christ of the Twenty-First Century* (Rockport, Mass.: Element Books, 1992).

2. Rosemary Haughton, *The Catholic Thing* (Springfield, Ill.: Templegate Publishers, 1979).

3. Ibid., 103–9.

4. For an interesting view of Eastern Christian spirituality which seems to echo Celtic spirituality, see George A. Maloney, SJ, *Gold, Frankincense and Myrrh: An Introduction to Eastern Christian Spirituality* (New York: Crossword, 1997).

5. Oliver Davies and Fiona Bowie, *Celtic Christian Spirituality: An Anthology of Medieval and Modern Sources* (New York: Continuum Publishing Co., 1995), 45. Copyright 1995 by Oliver Davies and Fiona Bowie. Reprinted with the permission of the Continuum Publishing Company.

Bibliography

I. Background on the Celts

Chadwick, Nora. *The Celts*. New York: Penguin Books, 1991.

Delaney, Frank. *The Celts*. London: HarperCollins, 1993.

Ellis, Peter Berresford. *The Druids*. Grand Rapids: Wm. B. Eerdmans, 1994.

————. *Celtic Women: Women in Celtic Society and Literature*. Grand Rapids: Wm. B. Eerdmans, 1996.

James, Simon. *The World of the Celts*. London: Thames and Hudson, 1993.

King, John. *The Celtic Druids' Year: Seasonal Cycles of the Ancient Celts*. London: Blanford, 1994.

Markale, Jean. *The Celts: Uncovering the Mythic and Historic Origins of Western Culture*. Rochester, Vt.: Inner Traditions International, 1993.

Matthews, Caitlin. *The Elements of the Celtic Tradition*. Rockport, Mass.: Element Books, 1991.

Megaw, Ruth and Vincent. *Celtic Art from the Beginnings to the Book of Kells*. London: Thames and Hudson, 1989.

O'Donnell, Robert, ed. *The Celtic Consciousness*. Symposium papers, Toronto, 1978. New York: George Braziller, 1981.

Pennick, Nigel. *Celtic Sacred Landscapes*. London: Thames and Hudson, 1996.

Sharkey, John. *The Celtic Mysteries: The Ancient Religion*. London: Thames and Hudson, 1975.

II. Celtic Christianity

Adam, David. *The Edge of Glory: Prayers in the Celtic Tradition*. Wilton, Conn.: Morehouse-Barlow, 1985.

————. *The Cry of the Deer: Meditations on the Hymn of St. Patrick*. Wilton, Conn.: Morehouse-Barlow, 1987.

Adomnan of Iona. *Life of St. Columba*. Trans. Richard Sharpe. London: Penguin Books, 1995.

Bamford, Christopher, and William Parker Marsh. *Celtic Christianity: Ecology and Holiness: An Anthology*. Hudson, N.Y.: Lindisfarne Press, 1982.

Bede. *The Ecclesiastical History of the English People*. Ed. Judith McClure and Roger Collins. New York: Oxford University Press, 1994.

Bitel, Lisa M. *Isle of the Saints: Monastic Settlements and Christian Community in Early Ireland*. Ithaca, N.Y.: Cornell University Press, 1990.

Bradley, Ian. *The Celtic Way.* London: Darton, Longman and Todd, 1993.

Carmichael, Alexander. *Carmina Gadelica: Hymns and Incantations.* Hudson, N.Y.: Lindisfarne Press, 1992.

Davies, Oliver, and Fiona Bowie, eds. *Celtic Christian Spirituality: An Anthology of Medieval and Modern Sources.* New York: Continuum, 1995.

De Paor, Liam. *Saint Patrick's World: The Christian Culture of Ireland's Apostolic Age.* Dublin: Four Courts Press, and Notre Dame, Ind.: University of Notre Dame Press, 1993.

De Paor, Maire, and Liam De Paor. *Early Christian Ireland.* London: Thames and Hudson, 1978.

de Waal, Esther, ed. *The Celtic Vision: Prayers and Blessings from the Outer Hebrides: Selections from the Carmina Gadelica.* Petersham, Mass.: St. Bede Press, 1988.

————. *Every Earthly Blessing: Rediscovering the Celtic Tradition: Celebrating a Spirituality of Creation.* Ann Arbor, Mich.: Servant Publications, 1992.

————. *The Celtic Way of Prayer: The Recovery of the Religious Imagination.* New York: Doubleday, 1997.

Duffy, Joseph. *Patrick in His Own Words.* Dublin: Veritas Publications, 1985.

Duncan, Anthony. *The Elements of Celtic Christianity.* Rockport, Mass.: Element Books, 1992.

Ellis, Peter Berresford. *Celtic Inheritance.* London: Constable Books, 1992.

Eriugena, John Scotus. *The Voice of the Eagle — The Heart of Celtic Christianity.* Trans. Christopher Bamford. Hudson, N.Y.: Lindisfarne Press, 1990.

Finney, John. *Recovering the Past: Celtic and Roman Mission.* London: Darton, Longman and Todd, 1996.

Harbison, Peter. *Pilgrimage in Ireland: The Monuments and the People.* Syracuse, N.Y.: Syracuse University Press, 1992.

Hughes, Kathleen, and Ann Hamlin. *Celtic Monasticism: The Modern Traveler to the Early Irish Church.* New York: Seabury Press, 1990.

Lehane, Brendan. *The Quest of Three Abbots: The Golden Age of Celtic Christianity (Patrick — Columba — Brendan).* Hudson, N.Y.: Lindisfarne Press, 1994.

Mackey, James, ed. *An Introduction to Celtic Christianity.* Edinburgh: T. & T. Clark, 1989.

MacReamoinn, Sean, ed. *The Church in a New Ireland.* Dublin: Columba Press, 1996.

Maher, Michael, ed. *Irish Spirituality.* Dublin: Veritas Publications, 1981.

Martnell, William. *Light from the West: The Irish Mission and the Emergence of Modern Europe.* New York: Crossword, 1978.

Mitton, Michael. *Restoring the Woven Cord: Strands of Celtic Christianity for the Church Today.* London: Darton, Longman and Todd, 1995.

O'Donoghue, Noel Dermot. *The Mountain behind the Mountain: Aspects of the Celtic Tradition.* Edinburgh: T. & T. Clark, 1993.

O'Dwyer, Peter. *Towards a History of Irish Spirituality.* Dublin: Columba Press, 1995.

O'Riordain, John J. *Irish Catholics: Tradition and Transition.* Dublin: Veritas Publications, 1980.

———. *The Music of What Happens: Celtic Spirituality: A View from the Inside.* Dublin: Columba Press, 1996.

Rodgers, Michael, and Marcus Losack. *Glendalough: A Celtic Pilgrimage.* Dublin: Columba Press, 1996.

Sellner, Edward. *Wisdom of the Celtic Saints.* Notre Dame, Ind.: Ave Maria Press, 1993.

Sheldrake, Philip. *Living between Two Worlds: Place and Journey in Celtic Spirituality.* Boston: Cowley Publications, 1995.

Toulson, Shirley. *The Celtic Year: A Month by Month Celebration of Celtic Christian Festivals and Sites.* Rockport, Mass.: Element Books, 1993.

Walsh, John R., and Thomas Bradley. *A History of the Irish Church 400–700 A.D.* Dublin: Columba Press, 1993.

Webb, J. F., trans. *The Age of Bede (Bede's Life of Cuthbert; Eddius Stephanus's Life of Wilfrid; Bede's Lives of the Abbots of Wearmouth and Jarrow; with the Voyage of St. Brendan).* Ed. D. H. Farmer. London: Penguin Books, 1988.

Whiteside, Lesley. *The Spirituality of St. Patrick.* Dublin: Columba Press, 1996.

III. *Other Books of Contemporary Interest*

Cahill, Thomas. *How the Irish Saved Civilization: The Untold Story of Ireland's Heroic Role from the Fall of Rome to the Rise of Medieval Europe.* New York: Doubleday, 1995.

Carney, James. *Medieval Irish Lyrics with the Irish Bards.* Dublin: Dolmen Press, 1985.

Condren, Mary. *The Serpent and the Goddess: Women, Religion and Power in Celtic Ireland.* San Francisco: Harper, 1989.

Ellis, Peter Berresford. *Hell or Connaught: The Cromwellian Colonisation of Ireland 1652–1660.* Belfast: Blackstaff Press, 1975.

Flower, Robin. *The Irish Tradition.* Dublin: Lilliput Press, 1994.

Jackson, Kenneth Hurlstone. *A Celtic Miscellany: Translations from the Celtic Literature.* London: Penguin Books, 1971.

O'Brien, Jacqueline, and Peter Harbison. *Ancient Ireland from Prehistory to the Middle Ages.* New York: Oxford University Press, 1996.

O'Donnell, Robert, ed. *The Celtic Consciousness.* Symposium papers, Toronto, 1978. New York: George Braziller, 1981.

O'Shea, Donagh. *Take Nothing for the Journey: Meditations on Time and Place.* Mystic, Conn.: Twenty-Third Publications, 1990.

Sheehy, Jeanne. *The Rediscovery of Ireland's Past: The Celtic Revival, 1830–1930.* London: Thames and Hudson, 1980.

IV. Other Resources

Anamchairde. A network of people interested in the Celtic spiritual tradition, 2374 Madison Road, Cincinnati, OH 45208.

Ballintubber Retreat Experience. Ballintubber Abbey, Claremorris, Co. Mayo, Ireland.

Celi De Teoranta. Programs in Celtic Spirituality. Castlekevin, Annamoe, Co. Wicklow, Ireland.

Celtic League. American Branch, P.O. Box 20153, Dag Hammarskjöld Postal Center, New York, NY 10017.

Celtic Spirituality Workshops and Retreats. Glastonbury Abbey Retreat Center, 16 Hull Street, Hingham, MA 02043.

Community of Aidan and Hilda. Red Hills Christian Centre, Snitterfield, Stratford-upon-Avon, Warwickshire, England CV37 0PQ.

Northumbria Community. Nether Springs at Hitton Hall, Chatton Alnwick, Northumberland, England NE66 5SD.

Saint Aidan Trust. P.O. Box 4241, Evergreen, CO 80437-4241.

Saint Aidan's Monastery (Hermitages). Dominican Sisters, Ferns, Co. Wexford, Ireland.

Index